READING
TIMOTHY
AND TITUS
with
JOHN STOTT

13 WEEKS FOR INDIVIDUALS OR GROUPS

JOHN STOTT
with DALE & SANDY LARSEN

IVP Connect

An imprint of InterVarsity Press
Downers Grove, Illinois

InterVarsity Press
P.O. Box 1400, Downers Grove, IL 60515-1426
ivpress.com
email@ivpress.com

This volume is abridged and edited from The Message of 1 Timothy & Titus ©1996 and The Message of 2 Timothy ©1973 by John R. W. Stott by permission of Inter-Varsity Press, England. Some of the discussion questions are from 1 Timothy & Titus ©1998 and 2 Timothy ©1998 by John R. W. Stott, originally published by InterVarsity Press, Downers Grove, Illinois, USA.

InterVarsity Press® is the book-publishing division of InterVarsity Christian Fellowship/USA®, a movement of students and faculty active on campus at hundreds of universities, colleges, and schools of nursing in the United States of America, and a member movement of the International Fellowship of Evangelical Students. For information about local and regional activities, visit intervarsity.org.

Cover design: Cindy Kiple
Interior design: Beth McGill
Images: © Jill Ferry / Trevillion Images

ISBN 978-0-8308-3196-8 (print)
ISBN 978-0-8308-9242-6 (digital)

Printed in the United States of America ∞

Library of Congress Cataloging-in-Publication Data
Names: Stott, John R. W., author.
Title: Reading Timothy and Titus with John Stott : 13 weeks for individuals
  or groups / John Stott, with Dale and Sandy Larsen.
Description: Downers Grove : InterVarsity Press, 2017. | Series: Reading the
  Bible with John Stott (RBJS)
Identifiers: LCCN 2017013145 (print) | LCCN 2017016959 (ebook) | ISBN
  9780830892426 (eBook) | ISBN 9780830831968 (pbk. : alk. paper)
Subjects: LCSH: Bible. Pastoral Epistles—Textbooks.
Classification: LCC BS2735.55 (ebook) | LCC BS2735.55 .S76 2017 (print) | DDC
  227/.830071—dc23
LC record available at https://lccn.loc.gov/2017013145

P	20	19	18	17	16	15	14	13	12	11	10	9	8	7	6	5	4	3	2	1
Y	33	32	31	30	29	28	27	26	25	24	23	22	21	20	19	18	17			

Contents

How to Read the Bible
with John Stott

During John Stott's life (1921–2011), he was one of the world's master Bible teachers. Christians on every continent heard and read John Stott's exposition of Scripture, which was at once instructive and inspiring. With over eight million copies of his more than fifty books sold in dozens of languages, it is not surprising that *Time* magazine recognized him in 2005 as one of the "100 Most Influential People in the World" and *Christianity Today* called him "evangelicalism's premier teacher and preacher." At the core of his ministry was the Bible and his beloved Bible Speaks Today series, which he originated as New Testament series editor. He himself contributed several volumes to the series, which have now been edited for this Reading the Bible with John Stott series.

The purpose of this series is to offer excerpts of Stott's *The Message of 1 Timothy & Titus* and *The Message of 2 Timothy* in brief readings, suitable for daily use. Though Stott was himself an able scholar, this series avoids technicalities and scholarly debates, with each reading emphasizing the substance, significance, and application of the text.

Following each set of six readings is found a discussion guide. This can be used by individuals to help them dig more deeply into the text. It can also be used by study groups meeting regularly. Individuals in the groups can go through the readings between group meetings and then use the discussion guide to help the group understand and apply the Scripture passage. Discussions are designed to last between forty-five and sixty minutes. Guidelines for leaders at the end of this volume offer many helpful suggestions for having a successful meeting.

If you are a group member, you can help everyone present in the following ways:

1. Read and pray through the readings before you meet.

2. Be willing to participate in the discussion. The leader won't be lecturing. Instead all will be asked to discuss what they have learned.

3. Stick to the topic being discussed. The focus is the particular passage of Scripture. Only rarely should you refer to other portions of the Bible or outside sources. This will allow everyone to participate on equal footing.

4. Listen attentively to what others have to say. Be careful not to talk too much but encourage a balanced discussion among all participants. You may be surprised by what you can learn from others. Generally, questions do not have one right answer but are intended to encourage various dimensions of the text.

5. Expect God to teach you through the passage and through what others have to say.

6. Use the following guidelines and read them at the start of the first session.

- We will make the group a safe place by keeping confidential what is said in the group about personal matters.

- We will provide time for each person to talk who wants to.

- We will listen attentively to each other.

- We will talk about ourselves and our own situations, avoiding conversation about others.

- We will be cautious about giving advice to one another.

John Stott had an immense impact on the church in the last half of the twentieth century. With these volumes readers today can continue to benefit from the riches of the Bible that Stott opened to millions.

Introduction

Paul's letters to Timothy and Titus have become known as the pastoral letters. The apostle's overriding preoccupation throughout all three letters is with the truth, that it may be faithfully guarded and handed on. The pertinence of this theme in our contemporary world is evident. Today people freely declare that there is no such thing as objective or universal truth; that all so-called truth is purely subjective, being culturally conditioned; and that therefore we all have our own truth, which has as much right to respect as anybody else's. Such thinking affirms the independent validity of every faith and ideology, and demands in shrill tones that we abandon as impossibly arrogant any attempt to convert somebody (let alone everybody) to our opinion.

In contrast to this relativizing of truth, it is wonderfully refreshing to read Paul's unambiguous commitment to it. As the apostle develops his thesis, we become aware of the existence of four groups of people and of the interplay between them: Paul and his fellow apostles, the false teachers, Timothy and Titus, and the pastors they are to select and appoint.

First there is Paul himself, who identifies himself at the beginning of all three letters as an apostle of Jesus Christ, adding in two of these letters that his apostleship is by the will or the command of God. All through these letters his self-conscious apostolic authority is apparent as he issues commands and expects obedience. Also, again and again, he refers to what he calls "the truth," "the faith," "the sound doctrine," "the teaching," or "the deposit." The plain implication is that a body of doctrine exists which, having been revealed and given by God, is objectively true. It is the teaching of the apostles. Paul constantly calls Timothy and Titus back to it, together with the churches they oversee.

Second, in opposition to Paul, there are false teachers. They are deviationists engaged in teaching what is alien to the teaching of the apostles. They have wandered and swerved from the faith. What they are spreading is not an alternative truth but falsehood.

Third, there are Timothy and Titus. They stand between the apostle and the church in the sense that they represent him and relay his teaching to the church. They have been appointed to oversee the churches in Ephesus and Crete respectively, yet their job specification has been written by Paul.

Fourth, there are the true and trustworthy pastors Timothy and Titus are to appoint. In both letters Paul lays down the conditions of eligibility they must fulfill. Apart from a consistent moral character and a Christian home life, they must also be loyal to the apostles' teaching and have a teaching gift so they will be able to both teach the truth and confute error.

Three stages of teaching lie behind the pastoral letters. These stages are clearly set out in 2 Timothy 2:2, where what Timothy has heard from Paul he is to "entrust to reliable people" (the pastors), who in turn will "also be qualified to teach others" (the churches). It is noteworthy that in this verse reliability to the Word and an ability to teach it are the two essential qualifications for the pastorate.

What makes doctrinal succession possible is that the teaching of the apostles was written down and has now been bequeathed to us in the New Testament. Just as Paul told Timothy to attend to Old Testament Scripture and to his written instructions, so we must do the same. For Paul is now permanently absent. His approaching death looms behind all three pastoral letters, especially behind 2 Timothy, in which he states explicitly that the time of his departure has come. So his paramount concern is to ensure the preservation of his teaching after his death. Now, Paul has been dead a long time. And there is no living apostle who can take his place. Instead, we have his writings. Indeed we have the whole Bible, both the Old and the New Testaments, the written legacy of the prophets and the apostles.

John Stott

1 Timothy 1

True or False?

❦

Threefold Greeting

1 TIMOTHY 1:1-2

> [1]Paul, an apostle of Christ Jesus by the command of God
> our Savior and of Christ Jesus our hope,
>
> [2]To Timothy my true son in the faith:
>
> Grace, mercy and peace from God the Father and
> Christ Jesus our Lord.

The beginning of Paul's first letter to Timothy is conventional.
Paul announces himself as the author, Timothy as his corre-
spondent, and God as the source of the grace, mercy, and peace
which Paul wishes Timothy to enjoy. He is not content, however,
with a bare greeting like "Paul to Timothy: Grace." Instead, each
of the three persons involved is elaborated.

As in nine of his thirteen New Testament letters, Paul designates himself "an apostle of Christ Jesus." Paul claims to be an
apostle of Christ on a level with the Twelve Jesus had named

"apostles," with all the teaching authority this represented. He was an apostle of Christ, chosen, called, appointed, equipped, and authorized directly by Christ. To put the matter beyond dispute or misunderstanding, Paul adds that God the Father was involved with Christ Jesus in commissioning him; it was by their command that he was an apostle.

Further, Paul locates his apostleship in a historical context whose beginning was the saving activity of "God our Savior" in the birth, death, and resurrection of Jesus and whose culmination will be "Christ Jesus our hope," his personal and glorious coming, which is the object of our Christian hope and which will bring down the curtain on history.

Paul then designates Timothy as "my true son in the faith." Spiritually, Timothy is Paul's genuine child, partly because he was responsible for his conversion and partly because Timothy has faithfully followed his teaching and example. By affirming Timothy's genuineness, Paul aims to reinforce his authority in the church.

After describing himself and Timothy, Paul refers to the God who binds them together in his family. What unites them is their common share in "grace, mercy and peace." Each word tells us something about the human condition. *Grace* is God's kindness to the guilty and undeserving, *mercy* is his pity on the wretched who cannot save themselves, and *peace* is his reconciliation of those who were previously alienated from him and from one another. All three issue from the same source: "God the Father and Christ Jesus our Lord." Father and Son are bracketed as the single source of divine blessing, as they were in verse 1 as the single author of the divine command which constituted Paul an apostle.

Misuse of the Law

1 TIMOTHY 1:3-7

> [3]As I urged you when I went into Macedonia, stay there in Ephesus so that you may command certain people not to teach false doctrines any longer [4]or to devote themselves to myths and endless genealogies. Such things promote controversial speculations rather than advancing God's work—which is by faith. [5]The goal of this command is love, which comes from a pure heart and a good conscience and a sincere faith. [6]Some have departed from these and have turned to meaningless talk. [7]They want to be teachers of the law, but they do not know what they are talking about or what they so confidently affirm.

Paul confirms an earlier appeal for Timothy to remain in Ephesus so that he might "command certain people not to teach false doctrines any longer." Who were these false teachers, and what were they teaching? Paul writes that they "want to be teachers of the law." There is actually a great need for Christian teachers of the moral law (the Ten Commandments as expounded by Jesus in the Sermon on the Mount), for it is through the teaching of the law that we come to a consciousness of our sin and learn the implications of loving our neighbor.

Evidently, then, there is both a right and a wrong, a legitimate and an illegitimate, use of the law. How are the false teachers misusing the law? Timothy is to command them not to "devote themselves to myths and endless genealogies." It seems that the false teaching was primarily a Jewish aberration. There was a kind of fanciful Jewish literature which rewrote and embellished Old Testament history, and Paul may be referring to these imaginative writings. At the same time, the law teachers are not the Judaizers Paul opposed in his letter to the Galatians and who taught salvation by obedience to the law. Instead, these people treat the law as a hunting ground for their conjectures. To Paul their approach is frivolous; God had given his law to his people for a much more serious purpose.

Paul indicates two consequences of the false teaching, which are enough in themselves to condemn it: it obstructs both faith and love. False teachings "promote controversial speculations rather than advancing God's work—which is by faith." Speculation raises doubts, while revelation evokes faith. "The goal of this command is love, which comes from a pure heart and a good conscience and a sincere faith." To depart from these things is to be caught up in "meaningless talk."

Thus Paul paints a double contrast: between speculation and faith in God's revelation, and between controversy and love for one another. Here are two practical tests for us to apply to all teaching. The first is the test of faith: Does it come from God, being in agreement with apostolic doctrine (so that it may be received by faith), or is it the product of fertile human imagination? The second is the test of love: Does it promote unity in the body of Christ, or if not (since truth itself can divide), is it irresponsibly divisive? The ultimate criteria by which to judge any teaching are whether it promotes the glory of God and the good of the church.

Law for Lawbreakers

1 TIMOTHY 1:8-11

> [8]We know that the law is good if one uses it properly. [9]We
> also know that the law is made not for the righteous but
> for lawbreakers and rebels, the ungodly and sinful, the
> unholy and irreligious, for those who kill their fathers or
> mothers, for murderers, [10]for the sexually immoral, for
> those practicing homosexuality, for slave traders and liars
> and perjurers—and for whatever else is contrary to the
> sound doctrine [11]that conforms to the gospel concerning
> the glory of the blessed God, which he entrusted to me.

Paul now turns from the wrong use of the law to its right use. He
sets his knowledge in contrast to the ignorance of the false
teachers. "We know that the law is good if one uses it properly.
We also know that law is made . . . for lawbreakers." Putting together these two truths "we know," we reach the striking
statement that the lawful use of the law is for the lawless. All law
is designed for those whose natural tendency is not to keep it but
to break it. It is only because as fallen human beings we have a
natural tendency to lawlessness that we need the law at all.

The statement that the law is "not for the righteous" cannot
refer to those who are righteous in the sense of "justified," since
Paul insists elsewhere that the justified do still need the law for
their sanctification. Nor can it be taken to mean that some
people exist who are so righteous that they do not need the law
to guide them, but only that some people think they are. "The
righteous" in these contexts means "the self-righteous."

Paul proceeds to illustrate the principle of "law for the lawless" with eleven examples of law-breaking. The first six words, which he sets in pairs, appear to be more general than specific. These clearly involve our duty to God and may refer to the first four of the Ten Commandments. The next five words are extremely specific in relation to our duty to our neighbor and evidently allude to commandments five to nine.

It is noteworthy that sins that contravene the law (as breaches of the Ten Commandments) are also contrary to the sound doctrine of the gospel. So the moral standards of the gospel do not differ from the moral standards of the law. We must not imagine that, because we have embraced the gospel, we may now repudiate the law.

To be sure, the law is impotent to save us, and we have been released from the law's condemnation, so that we are no longer "under" it in that sense. But God sent his Son to die for us and now puts his Spirit within us in order that the righteous requirement of the law may be fulfilled in us. There is no antithesis between law and gospel in the moral standards they teach; the antithesis is in the way of salvation, since the law condemns, while the gospel justifies.

Abundant Grace

1 TIMOTHY 1:12-14

[12]I thank Christ Jesus our Lord, who has given me strength, that he considered me trustworthy, appointing me to his service. [13]Even though I was once a blasphemer

and a persecutor and a violent man, I was shown mercy because I acted in ignorance and unbelief. [14]The grace of our Lord was poured out on me abundantly, along with the faith and love that are in Christ Jesus.

Turning from the false teachers and their misuse of the law, Paul now writes about himself and the gospel that has been entrusted to him. He retells the story of his conversion and commissioning, sandwiching it between two paeans of praise (the second to come in verse 17).

In particular Paul mentions three related blessings. First, "I thank Christ Jesus our Lord, who has given me strength." It is striking that he refers to the inner strength Christ has given him even before he specifies the ministry for which he needed to be strengthened. The appointment would have been inconceivable without the equipment. Second, he thanks Christ "that he considered me trustworthy." This cannot mean that Jesus Christ trusted Paul because he perceived him to be inherently trustworthy; Paul's fitness or faithfulness was due rather to the inner strength he had been promised. Third, he thanks Christ for "appointing me to his service." While Christian service takes many forms, Paul clearly refers to his commissioning as apostle to the Gentiles.

Paul gives further substance to his thanksgiving by reminding Timothy what he had been, how he received mercy, and why God had mercy on him. He uses three words to describe what he had been: "a blasphemer and a persecutor and a violent man." Perhaps the apostle intends to portray an ascending scale of evil from words (of blasphemy) through deeds (of persecution) to thoughts (of deep-seated hostility). When he opposed the gospel, he "acted in ignorance and unbelief." He is not saying that his ignorance established a claim on God's mercy (or mercy would no longer be mercy, nor would grace be grace), but only that his opposition was not open-eyed and willful.

Humanly speaking, there was no hope for someone as malicious and aggressive as Paul was. But he was not beyond the mercy of God.

To *mercy* Paul adds *grace*, which "was poured out on me abundantly." Grace overflowed like a river at flood stage, which bursts its banks and irresistibly carries everything before it. What the river of grace brought with it was not devastation but blessing, in particular "the faith and love that are in Christ Jesus." Grace flooded with faith a heart previously filled with unbelief and flooded with love a heart previously polluted with hatred. No wonder Paul's life is permeated with thanksgiving, not only for his salvation but also for the privilege of having been made an apostle of Christ.

A Trustworthy Saying

1 TIMOTHY 1:15-17

> [15]Here is a trustworthy saying that deserves full acceptance: Christ Jesus came into the world to save sinners—of whom I am the worst. [16]But for that very reason I was shown mercy so that in me, the worst of sinners, Christ Jesus might display his immense patience as an example for those who would believe in him and receive eternal life.

[17]Now to the King eternal, immortal, invisible, the only God, be honor and glory for ever and ever. Amen.

Paul quotes the first of the five "trustworthy sayings" that occur in the pastoral letters. On each occasion the saying is pithy, almost proverbial. Perhaps it is a familiar quotation from an early hymn or creed, to which Paul gives his own apostolic endorsement.

This "trustworthy saying" is a concise summary of the gospel. First, the content of the gospel is true and trustworthy, in distinction to the speculative nonsense of the false teachers. Second, the offer of the gospel is universal; it deserves to be accepted by all. Third, the essence of the gospel is that "Christ Jesus came into the world to save sinners." This statement alludes to both Christ's incarnation and his atonement. Fourth, the application of the gospel is personal. The universal offer is one thing; its individual acceptance is another.

What did Paul mean when he called himself "the worst of sinners"? He was so vividly aware of his own sins that he could not conceive that anybody could be worse. This is the language of every sinner whose conscience has been awakened and disturbed by the Holy Spirit.

If Paul's ignorant unbelief in the past was one reason why God had mercy on him, a second was related to the faith of others in the future, so that "Christ Jesus might display his immense patience as an example for those who would believe in him and receive eternal life." Although Paul's conversion had a number of unique features, it was also a prototype of all subsequent conversions because it was an exhibition of Christ's infinite patience. The conversion of Saul of Tarsus on the

Damascus road remains a standing source of hope to otherwise hopeless cases.

Paul breaks out into a spontaneous doxology in which he makes use of some phrases from an early liturgical form. He addresses God as "the King," the sovereign ruler of all things, who not only reigns over the natural order and the historical process but has also established his special kingdom through Christ and by the Spirit over his redeemed people. The divine King is "eternal," beyond the fluctuations of time. He is "immortal," beyond the ravages of decay and death. He is "invisible," beyond the limits of every horizon. No one has seen God, but his glory is displayed in the creation and reached its zenith in the incarnate Son. And he is "the only God." He has no rivals. To this great "King, eternal, immortal, invisible, the only God," Paul ascribes what is his due: "honor and glory for ever and ever." To this doxology all Christians can say "Amen."

Fight Well and Hold On

1 TIMOTHY 1:18-20

> [18]Timothy, my son, I am giving you this command in keeping with the prophecies once made about you, so that by recalling them you may fight the battle well, [19]holding on to faith and a good conscience, which some have rejected and so have suffered shipwreck with regard to the faith. [20]Among them are Hymenaeus and Alexander, whom I have handed over to Satan to be taught not to blaspheme.

Paul reminds Timothy both of the special father-son relationship that bound them together and of the circumstances of his ordination. Paul does not specify the "battle" Timothy is called to "fight well." Certainly to defend the revealed truth of God against those who deny or distort it is to engage in a dangerous and difficult fight that demands spiritual weapons. In particular, Timothy must keep "holding on to faith and a good conscience."

Timothy possesses two valuable things that he must carefully guard, an objective treasure called the "faith," meaning the apostolic faith, and a subjective one called "a good conscience." They need to be preserved together, which is what Hymenaeus and Alexander have failed to do. Having pushed away their conscience, they have shipwrecked their faith. Conversely, it is by preserving a good conscience that Timothy will be able to keep the faith. Thus belief and behavior, conviction and conscience, the intellectual and the moral, are closely linked. If we disregard the voice of conscience, allowing sin to remain unconfessed and unforsaken, our faith will not long survive.

So serious was the apostasy of Hymenaeus and Alexander that Paul writes of them: "whom I have handed over to Satan." This almost certainly means excommunication. Since the church is the dwelling place of God, it follows that to be ejected from it is to be sent back into the world, the habitat of Satan. Radical though this punishment is, it is not permanent or irrevocable. Its purpose is remedial, so the offenders may be "taught not to blaspheme." The implication is that, once the lesson has been learned, the excommunicated persons may be restored to the fellowship.

In this first chapter, which concerns the place of doctrine in the local church, Paul gives valuable instruction about false teaching. Its essential nature is that it is a deviation from revealed truth. Its damaging results are that it replaces faith with speculation and love with dissension. Its fundamental cause is the rejection of a good conscience before God. In the face of such a situation, Timothy is to stay at his post and to fight well, both demolishing error and contending earnestly for the truth.

1 Timothy 1

DISCUSSION GUIDE

OPEN

When is it difficult for you to practice God's truth instead of being less than honest?

STUDY

Read 1 Timothy 1.

1. From this first section of his letter to Timothy, what do we learn about Paul?

2. What false teachings did Paul point out for Timothy?

3. What do verses 6-7 tell us about the nature and consequences of false teaching?

4. Paul writes that the goal of true teaching is love. How do purity, a clean conscience, and faith manifest themselves in love?

5. In contrast to false teaching, Paul affirmed the right use of the law. What is it?

6. Why is it so important to maintain sound doctrine and refute false teachings?

7. What false teachings do Christians have to guard against today? Identify several specific examples.

8. For what did Paul express gratitude to God, and why?

9. In this passage Paul offers a before-and-after picture of himself. How would you describe Paul before and after he became a believer?

10. Why did Christ show Paul mercy?

11. How was Paul an example of Christ's "immense patience"?

12. Paul urged Timothy to "fight the battle well." What part do faith and a good conscience play in engaging in this battle?

13. How does this battle play out in your own life?

APPLY

1. How are you an example so others will believe in Christ?

2. In what areas do you need to change to be a better example?

1 Timothy 2
Worship and Women

❦

Pray for All

1 TIMOTHY 2:1-2

> ¹I urge, then, first of all, that petitions, prayers, intercession and thanksgiving be made for all people—²for kings and all those in authority, that we may live peaceful and quiet lives in all godliness and holiness.

As Paul had "urged" Timothy to remain in Ephesus to combat error, so now he exhorts him to give priority to public worship. The church is essentially a worshiping, praying community. This emphasis on the priority of worship has particular importance for us who are called evangelical people. For whenever we fail to take public worship seriously, we are less than the fully biblical Christians we claim to be. I sometimes wonder whether the comparatively slow progress toward peace and justice in the world and toward world evangelization is due more than anything else to the prayerlessness of the people of God.

Paul mentions four different kinds of worship: *petitions*, *prayers*, *intercession*, and *thanksgiving*. Although Paul uses this cluster of four words, they all focus on a single theme, namely, that they should "be made for all people." In particular, Paul directs the churches to pray "for kings and all those in authority." This is a remarkable instruction, since at that time no Christian ruler existed anywhere in the world. The reigning emperor was Nero, whose vanity, cruelty, and hostility to the Christian faith were widely known. The persecution of the church, spasmodic at first, was soon to become systematic, and Christians were understandably apprehensive. Yet they had recourse to prayer.

Paul is quite specific in directing why the church should pray for national leaders. It is first and foremost "that we may live peaceful and quiet lives." The basic benefit of good government is peace, meaning freedom both from war and from civil strife. Paul had many experiences of this blessing when Roman officials intervened on his behalf.

Prayer for peace is not to be dismissed as selfish. Its motivation can be altruistic, for only within an ordered society is the church free to fulfill its God-given responsibilities without hindrance. Two blessings of peace are mentioned, "godliness and holiness," and a third (the propagation of the gospel) is implied. *Godliness* is a favorite word in Paul's pastoral letters, where it means the worship of God or religious devotion. *Holiness* in this context seems to mean moral wholeheartedness.

What stands out in this passage is the universal range of the church's responsibility. Because God's purpose and Christ's death concern everybody, the church's prayers and proclamation must concern everybody too.

God's Desire for All

1 TIMOTHY 2:3-4

> ³This is good, and pleases God our Savior, ⁴who wants all people to be saved and to come to a knowledge of the truth.

"This" is prayer that those in authority will maintain peace. Here Paul implies another positive benefit of peace, which is that peaceful conditions facilitate the propagation of the gospel. The ultimate object of our prayers for national leaders, then, is that in the context of the peace they preserve, religion and morality can flourish, and evangelism can go forward without interruption.

The reason the church should reach out and embrace all people in its prayers is that this is the compass of God's desire. We need to repent of the monopolizing spirit of racism, nationalism, tribalism, classism, and parochialism, and the pride and prejudice that are the cause of these narrow horizons. The truth is that God loves the whole world, desires all people to be saved, and so commands us to preach the gospel to all the nations and to pray for their conversion.

Scripture unquestionably teaches divine election both in the Old Testament and in the New Testament, yet this truth must never be expressed in such a way as to deny the complementary truth that God wants all people to be saved. Election is usually introduced in Scripture to humble us (reminding us that the credit for our salvation belongs to God alone) or to reassure us (promising us that God's love will never let us go) or to stir us to mission (recalling that God chose Abraham and his family in order to bless all the families of the earth through him). Election is never introduced in order to contradict the universal offer of the gospel or to provide us with an excuse for opting out of world evangelization. If some are excluded, it is because they exclude themselves by rejecting the gospel offer. As for God, he "wants all people to be saved."

Wherever we look in Scripture we see paradox: divine sovereignty and human responsibility, universal offer and electing purpose, the all and the some, the cannot and the will not. The right response is neither to seek superficial harmonization by manipulating some part of the evidence nor to declare that Jesus and Paul contradicted themselves, but to affirm both parts of the antinomy as true, while humbly confessing that at present our little minds are unable to resolve it.

One God, One Mediator

1 TIMOTHY 2:5-6

> [5]For there is one God and one mediator between God and mankind, the man Christ Jesus, [6]who gave himself as a ransom for all people. This has now been witnessed to at the proper time.

A mediator is an intermediary, the person in the middle who effects a reconciliation between two rival parties. Between God and the human race, Paul writes, there is only "one mediator," Jesus. His unique qualifications as mediator are to be found in his person and work, in who he is and what he has done.

First, the person of Jesus is unique. He is God from the beginning, deriving his divine being from his Father eternally, and he became human in the womb of his mother, Mary, deriving his human being from her in time. Thus the New Testament bears witness to him as the unique God-man. There is no parallel anywhere else.

Second, the work of Jesus is unique, in particular what he did when he died on the cross. He "gave himself as a ransom for all people." Note the apostle's remarkable leap from the birth of Jesus ("the man Christ Jesus") to his death ("who gave himself"). The one led to the other. He was born to die. His death is portrayed as both a sacrifice (he "gave himself") and a "ransom." A ransom was the price paid for the release of slaves or captives. Still in our day hijackers hold people for ransom. The word implies that we were in bondage to sin and judgment, unable to save ourselves, and that the price paid for our deliverance was the death of Christ in our place.

Here is the double uniqueness of Jesus Christ, which qualifies him to be the only mediator. First there is the uniqueness of his divine-human person, and second the uniqueness of his substitutionary, redeeming death. We must keep these three nouns together—the *man*, the *ransom*, and the *mediator*. Historically, they refer to the three major events in his saving career: his birth, by which he became *man*; his death, in which he gave himself as a *ransom*; and his exaltation (by resurrection and ascension) to the Father's right hand, where he acts as our *mediator* or advocate today. Theologically, they refer to the three great doctrines of salvation: the incarnation, the atonement, and the heavenly mediation.

Since in no other person but Jesus of Nazareth has God first become man (taking our humanity to himself) and then given himself as a ransom (taking our sin and guilt upon himself), therefore he is the only mediator. There is no other. No one else possesses, or has ever possessed, the necessary qualifications to mediate between God and sinners.

Heralds and Teachers

1 TIMOTHY 2:7

> [7]And for this purpose I was appointed a herald and an apostle—I am telling the truth, I am not lying—and a true and faithful teacher of the Gentiles.

How are we to understand the three nouns *herald, apostle,* and *teacher*? Paul was all three, but nobody is all three today. The designation "apostle," when used of the "apostles of Christ" in distinction to the "apostles of the churches," alluded primarily to the Twelve, to whom Paul and James were later added. They were eyewitnesses of the historic Jesus, especially of his resurrection, were promised the special inspiration of the Holy Spirit and were given authority to teach in Christ's name. In addition, Paul was appointed the "apostle to the Gentiles." His strong ejaculation that he was telling the truth and not lying was probably necessary because the false teachers were challenging his apostolic authority.

Although there are no "apostles" of Christ today who are comparable in inspiration and authority to the writers of the New Testament, there are certainly "heralds" and "teachers." It was the task of the apostles to formulate, defend, and commend the gospel. It is the task of heralds to proclaim it and the task of teachers to give systematic instruction in its doctrines and ethics. What do they proclaim and teach? Jesus Christ, the God-man, the ransom and the mediator, and all that is implied by those truths. To whom do they minister? To "the Gentiles," all people of all nations. How do they do so? By being "true and faithful."

Today there is an urgent need for such heralds and teachers. It is not enough that the Son of God was born, died, and was raised, or that he is the uniquely qualified God-man, ransom, and mediator; this great good news must be made known, both heralded and taught, throughout the world.

The universal concern of the church arises from the universal concern of God. Because there is one God and one mediator, all people must be included in the church's prayers and proclamation. It is the unity of God and the uniqueness of Christ that demand the universality of the gospel. God's desire and Christ's death concern all people; therefore the church's duty concerns all people too, reaching out to them in both earnest prayer and urgent witness.

Prayer and Good Deeds

1 TIMOTHY 2:8-10

> [8]Therefore I want the men everywhere to pray, lifting up holy hands without anger or disputing. [9]I also want the women to dress modestly, with decency and propriety, adorning themselves, not with elaborate hairstyles or gold or pearls or expensive clothes, [10]but with good deeds, appropriate for women who profess to worship God.

Continuing to address the topic of public worship, Paul turns from the priority and scope of the local church's prayers to the respective roles and appropriate behavior of men and women whenever the church assembles for worship. We cannot isolate Paul's words from Scripture's fundamental assertion of the equal value and dignity of men and women by creation and redemption. There is no difference between the sexes either in the divine image we bear or in our status as God's children through faith in Christ. Every idea of gender superiority or inferiority is ruled out from the start.

We have to discern in Scripture between God's essential revelation (which is changeless) and its cultural expression (which is changeable). Then we are in a position to preserve the former as permanent and universal, and to transpose the latter into contemporary cultural terms.

Always and everywhere men are to pray in holiness and love. Expressed negatively, three hindrances to prayer are unholiness, anger, and disputing. So holiness, love, and peace are indispensable to prayer. But is the lifting up of hands equally essential? No, bodily postures and gestures in prayer are cultural, and a wide range of variations occurs in Scripture. Whether we stand, sit, bow down, kneel, or fall on our faces, and whether our hands are lifted, spread, folded, clasped, clapping, or waving are matters of little consequence—although we do need to make sure that our posture is both appropriate to our culture and genuinely expressive of our inward devotion.

Always and everywhere women are to "dress modestly, with decency and propriety." It is not possible to distinguish these words from one another in a clear-cut way. But the general impression is clear, that women are to be discreet and modest in their dress and not to wear any garment that is deliberately suggestive or seductive. This establishes a universal principle. There is no biblical warrant in these verses for women to neglect their appearance. The question is how they should adorn themselves: "with good deeds, appropriate for women who profess to worship God." This is the beauty of Christlikeness.

Women's Roles in the Fellowship

1 TIMOTHY 2:11-15

> [11] A woman should learn in quietness and full submission.
> [12] I do not permit a woman to teach or to assume authority over a man; she must be quiet. [13] For Adam was formed first, then Eve. [14] And Adam was not the one deceived; it was the woman who was deceived and became a sinner.
> [15] But women will be saved through childbearing—if they continue in faith, love and holiness with propriety.

Paul offers two complementary instructions to or about women. Positively, "a woman should learn in quietness and full submission." Negatively, she is not "to teach or to assume authority over a man." A woman's behavior in public worship is to be characterized by quietness or silence, not teaching, and by submission, not authority.

A Christian mind schooled in the perspectives and presuppositions of the New Testament knows that its ethical commands and their cultural expressions are not equally normative and must therefore be distinguished. So in verse 8 holiness and love are ethical, but hand lifting is cultural, and in verses 9-10 decency and modesty are ethical, while hairstyles and jewelry are cultural. Why should we not find the same distinction between the ethical and the cultural in verses 11-12? The context (with its three regulations about prayers, adornment, and submission) should at least open us to this possibility.

It seems to me that Paul's instructions cover only the universal principle of female submission to male headship and not its changeable cultural expression. As men should pray in holiness, love, and peace, but not necessarily lift up their hands while they do so; and as women should adorn themselves with modesty, decency, and good works, but not necessarily abstain from all hair plaiting, gold, and pearls; so women should submit to the headship (caring responsibility) of men and not try to reverse sexual roles, but not necessarily refrain from teaching them.

Paul supplies a biblical basis for what he has written. He looks back to Adam and Eve, the original human pair. His argument for male headship rests on the facts of the creation and the fall. But what do we make of Paul's mysterious promise: "women will be saved through childbearing"? The best explanation is that women will be saved through the birth of the Child, referring to Christ. By this rendering, "saved" has a spiritual connotation, "through" is the means by which salvation comes, and the definite article before "childbearing" in the Greek sentence is explained. Earlier in the chapter (verse 5) the "one mediator between God and mankind" has been identified as "the man Christ Jesus," who of course became a human being by being born of a woman. Further, in the context of Paul's references to the creation and fall, a reference to the promised redemption through the woman's seed (Genesis 3:15) would be most apt. The serpent had deceived Eve; her posterity (Christ) would defeat him.

1 Timothy 2

....

Discussion Guide

OPEN

What role does worship play in your spiritual life?

STUDY

1. Paul begins his instructions about public worship with prayer, stating that it is first in importance. Why is it so important?

2. What various kinds of prayer does Paul mention in this passage?

3. Verse 2 tells us to pray "for kings and all those in authority." Who would be the equivalent of these people in your country today?

4. Why are we to pray for them?

5. In linking prayer with salvation, what aspects of salvation does Paul highlight in verses 3-7?

6. How is the truth about Jesus in verses 5-6 challenged today?

7. Verses 8-15 have been interpreted in a variety of ways and

have caused numerous arguments about the roles of men and women in the church. One rule of interpretation is to discern between universal instructions/principles and cultural expressions of them. Looking at the passage from this perspective, identify the universal instructions, the cultural expressions in Paul's day, and the cultural expressions for today.

8. Why did Paul focus on anger and disputing in connection with prayer?

9. When have you found sinful attitudes interfering with your prayers?

10. What steps can you take to broaden the scope of your prayers?

11. If Paul were writing this letter to your church today, what might he say about the roles of men and women?

APPLY

1. Consider the fact that God "wants all people to be saved and to come to a knowledge of the truth" (v. 4). How will this affect your interaction with people this week?

3

1 Timothy 3

A Leader to Follow

❦

Overseer Qualifications

1 TIMOTHY 3:1-7

[1]Here is a trustworthy saying: Whoever aspires to be an overseer desires a noble task. [2]Now the overseer is to be above reproach, faithful to his wife, temperate, self-controlled, respectable, hospitable, able to teach, [3]not given to drunkenness, not violent but gentle, not quarrelsome, not a lover of money. [4]He must manage his own family well and see that his children obey him, and he must do so in a manner worthy of full respect. [5](If anyone does not know how to manage his own family, how can he take care of God's church?) [6]He must not be a recent convert, or he may become conceited and fall under the same judgment as the devil. [7]He must also have a good reputation with outsiders, so that he will not fall into disgrace and into the devil's trap.

From the importance of apostolic doctrine (chap. 1) and the conduct of public worship (chap. 2), Paul turns to the pastoral oversight of the church and the necessary qualifications of pastors (chap. 3). This remains a vital topic in every place and generation, for the health of the church depends largely on the quality, faithfulness, and teaching of its ordained ministers.

Paul begins with "a trustworthy saying: Whoever aspires to be an overseer desires a noble task." He does not condone a selfish ambition for the prestige and power associated with the ordained ministry. Rather he recognizes that the pastorate is "a noble task" because it involves the care and nurture of the people of God. It is laudable to desire this privilege.

But isn't becoming a pastor a matter of divine call rather than human aspiration? Yes, elsewhere Paul clearly affirms the call and appointment of God. So the selection of candidates for the pastorate entails three essentials: the call of God, the inner aspiration and conviction of the individuals concerned, and their conscientious screening by the church as to whether they meet the requirements that the apostle now goes on to list. As Paul proceeds from the general to the particular, we can compile a kind of questionnaire for a candidate for the pastorate. It is interesting that the selection procedure of many churches today does not include an examination of candidates in these ten areas. They constitute a necessary, comprehensive, and challenging test.

In the middle of a series of moral qualities, Paul mentions one "professional" qualification: "able to teach." It follows from this that pastors are essentially teachers. What distinguishes Christian pastoral ministry is the preeminence of the Word of

God. The fact that overseers must have a teaching gift shows that the church has no liberty to ordain anyone God has not called and gifted.

Deacon Qualifications

1 TIMOTHY 3:8-10

> [8]In the same way, deacons are to be worthy of respect, sincere, not indulging in much wine, and not pursuing dishonest gain. [9]They must keep hold of the deep truths of the faith with a clear conscience. [10]They must first be tested; and then if there is nothing against them, let them serve as deacons.

Because of other uses of the Greek word from which we get "deacon," it is understandable that deacons are thought to have specialized in practical administration and ministry. But the requirement of verse 9, that the deacons have a strong and steadfast grasp of the revealed faith, suggests that they were expected to teach it, which was the chief responsibility of the overseers.

Paul emphasizes four areas in which deacons should be qualified.

First, deacons must have self-mastery. In their behavior, speech, use of alcohol, and attitude to money, candidates for the diaconate are to have control of themselves.

Second, deacons must have orthodox convictions. They are to maintain "a clear conscience," holding on to God's revelation with sincere and strong conviction.

Third, deacons must have been tested and approved. In addition to the selection procedure Paul has been outlining, there needs to be a period of probation in which the congregation may assess the character, beliefs, and gifts of the candidates for the diaconate. It is right that in this way the congregation is given a share in the testing of potential deacons.

Fourth, deacons must have an irreproachable home life, which we will see implied in verses 11-12.

So then, rather than distinguishing deacons from overseers as distinguishing social workers from teachers, it is better to think of the deacons as assisting the overseers in their ministry. The phrase "in the same way" shows that the qualifications for deacons overlap with those for overseers.

Words for Women

1 TIMOTHY 3:11

> ¹¹In the same way, the women are to be worthy of respect, not malicious talkers but temperate and trustworthy in everything.

Literally this verse begins "Women likewise . . .". Commentators are not agreed whether these women are deacons' wives or female deacons, for the word could apply to either.

In favor of female deacons, "in the same way" of verse 11, like that of verse 8, leads us to expect a new category. It would be strange for deacons' wives to be mentioned when elders' wives are not. There is no "their" before "women," which would be necessary if it meant "their wives." And we know from Phoebe (Romans 16:1) that there were women deacons at this time.

In favor of "deacons' wives," on the other hand, these women are not designated "deacons" like Phoebe. The reference to them is sandwiched between two references to deacons, which would make an allusion to their wives quite natural. And the omission of a reference to the women's married faithfulness, corresponding to verses 2 and 12, would be explained if these women were the deacons' wives.

Commentators are still divided on this question. One or two suggest that it could be a reference to both, since wives and female deacons could share in assisting the male deacons in their ministry.

In either case, these women are to be "worthy of respect" like the deacons in verse 8. They are not to be "malicious talkers." By contrast, having control of their tongue, they are to be "temperate" like the overseers in verse 2 and are to be "trustworthy in everything." These women, however they are identified, have a place of importance and responsibility in the life of the church.

The Outcome of Faithful Service

1 TIMOTHY 3:12-13

> [12]A deacon must be faithful to his wife and must manage his children and his household well. [13]Those who have served well gain an excellent standing and great assurance in their faith in Christ Jesus.

Paul now reverts to a discussion of deacons. Whether or not verse 11 refers to deacons' wives, "a deacon must be faithful to his wife and must manage his children and his household well," just like the candidate for overseer (vv. 2, 4, 5).

"Those who have served well" in the diaconate will gain two things. The first is "an excellent standing." This can denote a step, stair, grade, or rank. In this case the "standing" will be spiritual, either a position of honor in the esteem of God and the church, or even a step forward in their spiritual journey. The second thing faithful deacons gain is "great assurance in their faith in Christ Jesus." This assurance denotes freedom of speech or boldness before God or human beings. Faithful service will increase their Christian confidence.

Looking back, it is clear that the qualifications for overseers and deacons are very similar. There is a core of Christian qualities that all Christian leaders should exhibit.

Putting the two lists together, we note that there are five main areas to be investigated. In regard to themselves, candidates must be self-controlled and mature, including in the areas of drink, money, temper, and tongue. In regard to family, they must be faithful in marriage and able to discipline their children. In regard to relationships, they must be hospitable and gentle. In regard to outsiders, they must be highly esteemed. And in regard to the faith, they must be strong in their hold on its truth and gifted in teaching it.

There is plenty of material in this chapter both to encourage the right people to offer for pastoral ministry and to discourage the wrong ones from doing so. The discouragement is that the required standards are high and the task is arduous. The responsibility of caring for God's church is calculated to daunt the best and the most gifted Christians. But the corresponding encouragement is that the pastorate is a noble task, a beautiful undertaking, a laudable ambition. It involves giving oneself to the service of others.

The words *overseer* and *deacon* are both applied to the Lord Jesus in the New Testament. Could there be any greater honor than to follow in his footsteps and share in part of his roles as overseer and deacon that he is willing to delegate to us?

Interim Instructions

1 TIMOTHY 3:14-15

> [14]Although I hope to come to you soon, I am writing you these instructions so that, [15]if I am delayed, you will know how people ought to conduct themselves in God's household, which is the church of the living God, the pillar and foundation of the truth.

From the qualifications for the pastorate, Paul turns to the church in which pastors serve. For the nature of the ministry is determined by the nature of the church.

Paul uses three descriptive expressions of the church, each of which illustrates a different aspect of it: "God's household" or family, "the church of the living God," and "the pillar and foundation of the truth."

God's household. By new birth of the Spirit we become members of the family of God, related to him as our Father and to all fellow believers as our sisters and brothers. As God's children we have an equal dignity before him, irrespective of age, sex, race, or culture; as sisters and brothers we are called to love, forbear, and support one another, enjoying in fact the rich "one anotherness" or reciprocity of the Christian fellowship.

The church of the living God. In the Old Testament, the Lord is named "the living God" in contrast to the lifeless idols of the heathen. The essence of God's covenant promise to Israel was that he would dwell among them and be their God, and they would be his people. An even more vivid consciousness of the presence of the living God should characterize the Christian church today. We are the temple of the living God. In our worship we bow down before the living God. Through the reading and exposition of his Word we hear his voice addressing us. We meet him at his Table, when he makes himself known to us through the breaking of bread. In our fellowship we love each other as he has loved us. And our witness becomes bolder and more urgent.

The pillar and foundation of the truth. A foundation or buttress stabilizes a building. Just so, the church is responsible to hold the truth steady against the storms of heresy and unbelief. The purpose of pillars, however, is not only to hold the roof firm, but to thrust it high so that it can be clearly seen even from a distance. As pillars lift a building high while remaining themselves unseen, so the church's function is not to advertise itself but to advertise and display the truth. To hold the truth firm is the defense and confirmation of the gospel; to hold it high is the proclamation of the gospel. The church is called to both these ministries.

The Mystery of Godliness

1 TIMOTHY 3:16

> [16]Beyond all question, the mystery from which true godliness springs is great:

> He appeared in the flesh,
>   was vindicated by the Spirit,
> was seen by angels,
>   was preached among the nations,
> was believed on in the world,
>   was taken up in glory.

What is the truth that the church must both guard against every distortion and falsification, and proclaim without fear or compromise throughout the world? It concerns Jesus Christ, to whom Paul now bears witness by quoting from an early hymn or creed.

The liturgical statement Paul quotes consists of six lines that closely resemble one another stylistically. What do the six statements mean, and how do they relate to one another? The best suggestion is that the hymn consists of three couplets, in each of which there is a deliberate antithesis: between flesh and spirit, between angels and nations, between world and glory.

The first couplet speaks of the revelation of Christ ("he appeared in the flesh, was vindicated by the Spirit"). Here are the human and divine aspects of his earthly life and ministry in Palestine.

The second couplet speaks of the witnesses of Christ ("was seen by angels, was preached among the nations"). Now the significance of Jesus Christ is seen to extend far beyond Palestine to all the inhabitants of heaven and earth, to angels as well as humans, to the nations as well as the Jews.

The third couplet speaks of the reception Christ was given ("was believed on in the world, was taken up in glory"). For heaven and earth did more than see and hear him; they joined in giving him recognition and acclaim.

The mystery of godliness that the church proclaims, the truth of which the church is the foundation and pillar, is the historic yet cosmic Christ.

In conclusion, Paul's perspective in this chapter is to view the overseers and the deacons in the light of the church they are called to serve, and to view the church in the light of the truth it is called to confess. One of the surest roads to the reform and renewal of the church is to recover a grasp of its essential identity as "God's household, . . . the church of the living God, *and* the pillar and foundation of the truth."

1 Timothy 3

....

DISCUSSION GUIDE

OPEN

What qualifications did you need for your current job or a past job? Why were they necessary?

STUDY

1. This passage begins with the second "trustworthy saying" in the pastoral letters, focusing on the overseer, also called pastor or elder. Why is being an overseer a "noble task"?

2. In verses 1-7 Paul lists a number of qualifications for pastor. Take a look at these qualifications, considering which are character qualities and which are abilities. Note why each is important for leaders.

3. From the list of qualifications for deacons (vv. 8-13), develop a questionnaire to use with potential candidates for this position. Include a definition or description of each qualification as well as an example.

4. Verse 11 literally begins "Women likewise." Commentators do not agree on whether these women are the

deacons' wives or female deacons, since the word can apply to either. In either case, what character qualities did Paul say they should possess?

5. Describe the reward for serving well as a deacon (v. 13).

6. From verses 14-16, how would you summarize Paul's purpose for writing this letter?

7. How does Paul describe the church (v. 15)?

8. What does each of these word pictures convey about the church?

9. In verse 16 Paul describes Christ with a series of affirmations. What do they teach about him?

10. How do these statements build on one another?

APPLY

1. Think about the leadership roles you currently have (for example: parent, supervisor, committee chairperson, Bible study leader). How do you measure up to the leadership qualifications listed in this chapter?

2. Which qualification do you want to cultivate or deepen in your life, and what specific steps will you take to do so?

4

1 Timothy 4:1–5:2
Choose Your Weapons

❧

The Causes of Error

1 Timothy 4:1-2

> ¹The Spirit clearly says that in later times some will abandon the faith and follow deceiving spirits and things taught by demons. ²Such teachings come through hypocritical liars, whose consciences have been seared as with a hot iron.

In spite of the church's role as the guardian of the truth, "some will abandon the faith." Paul says that this Christian apostasy will take place "in later times," but he quickly slips from the future tense into the present, indicating his belief that the "later times" have already begun.

On the surface the situation is quite straightforward. Certain teachers begin to spread their erroneous views, and some gullible people listen to them, are taken in by them, and in consequence abandon the apostolic faith. But Paul looks beneath this surface appearance and explains to Timothy the underlying spiritual dynamic.

The first cause of error is diabolical. Those who "abandon the faith" do so because they have been following "deceiving spirits and things taught by demons." Speaking under the influence of the Spirit of truth, Paul declares the false teachers to be under the influence of deceiving spirits. We do not take this fact sufficiently seriously. Scripture portrays the devil not only as the tempter, enticing people into sin, but also as the deceiver, seducing people into error. Why do intelligent and educated people swallow the fantastic speculations of various false religions and philosophies? It is because there is not only a Spirit of truth but also a spirit of falsehood.

Second, error has a human cause. The devil does not usually deceive people directly. Ideas inspired by demons gain an entry into the world and the church through human agents. False teachers, although seduced by deceiving spirits, are themselves intentional deceivers, however misleading their mask of learning and religion may be. They do not themselves believe what they are teaching.

The third and most basic cause of error is moral. The hypocritical lies of the false teachers are now traced back to the violation of their "consciences," which have been "seared as with a hot iron." Their consciences have been cauterized and therefore anesthetized and deadened, so that the voice of conscience is smothered and eventually silenced.

The grim sequence of events in the career of the false teachers has now been revealed. It is a perilous downward path from the deaf ear and the cauterized conscience to the deliberate lie, the deception of demons, and the ruination of others. It begins when we tamper with our conscience rather than keeping our conscience clear.

A Theological Test: Creation

1 TIMOTHY 4:3-5

> [3]They forbid people to marry and order them to abstain from certain foods, which God created to be received with thanksgiving by those who believe and who know the truth. [4]For everything God created is good, and nothing is to be rejected if it is received with thanksgiving, [5]because it is consecrated by the word of God and prayer.

It is clear that the false teaching in Ephesus consisted of a false asceticism: "They forbid people to marry and order them to abstain from certain foods." Marriage and food relate to the two most basic appetites of the human body: sex and hunger. They are natural appetites, although both can be abused by degenerating into lust and greed.

Where does the essence of the false teachers' error lie? And how can it be detected? Paul supplies two fundamental tests, which are widely applicable. The first is a theological test, the doctrine of creation.

Marriage and certain foods, which the false teachers were forbidding, are gifts "which God created to be received with thanksgiving by those who believe and who know the truth." How can anybody despise marriage, let alone forbid it, when

God instituted it? How can anybody command abstention from certain foods, when God created them to be received with thanksgiving? What God has made and given us, we are to receive and thank him for.

The principle is given a universal application: "For everything God created is good, and nothing is to be rejected if it is received with thanksgiving." If everything was declared good by creation, then nothing is to be declared taboo. This is assuredly an allusion to the refrain of Genesis 1 that everything God made was good. Paul clinches the argument: "because it is consecrated by the word of God and prayer."

Thus marriage and food, and all God's many other creation gifts, are consecrated twice over, first and foremost objectively in themselves, since God made or instituted them, gave them to us to enjoy, and has said so in Scripture. Then, second, they are consecrated to us subjectively when we recognize their divine origin and receive them from God with gratitude.

Notice Paul does not say that "everything is good," but that "everything God created is good." Not everything that exists has come unsullied from the Creator's hand. The creation was followed by the fall, which introduced evil into the world and spoiled much of God's good creation. We therefore need discernment to know what in our human experience is attributable to the creation and what to the fall. A flagrant current misuse of the creation argument is the claim that the practices of heterosexual and homosexual people are equally good because they are equally created. It is no more appropriate to celebrate homosexuality than other disordered human tendencies that are due to the fall, such as our irrationality, covetousness, or pride. We must be careful not to confuse creation and fall, order and disorder, but rather to ensure that we celebrate only what God created, and gratefully receive only what he gives.

An Ethical Test: Godliness

1 TIMOTHY 4:6-10

> ⁶If you point these things out to the brothers and sisters, you will be a good minister of Christ Jesus, nourished on the truths of the faith and of the good teaching that you have followed. ⁷Have nothing to do with godless myths and old wives' tales; rather, train yourself to be godly. ⁸For physical training is of some value, but godliness has value for all things, holding promise for both the present life and the life to come. ⁹This is a trustworthy saying that deserves full acceptance. ¹⁰That is why we labor and strive, because we have put our hope in the living God, who is the Savior of all people, and especially of those who believe.

Paul's first test of the false asceticism in Ephesus was the doctrine of creation. His second one is an ethical test, the priority of godliness.

Paul makes it plain that it is "the good teaching" which makes "a good minister," in two ways: that he both instructs people in it and nourishes himself on it, "nourished on the truths of the faith and of the good teaching that you have followed." Behind the ministry of public teaching there lies the discipline of private study. All the best teachers have themselves remained students. They teach well because they learn well.

With verse 7 the metaphor changes from the nourishment of a child to the exercise of an athlete: "train yourself to be godly." The basic meaning of *godliness* is "respect" or "reverence." In the New Testament it is used exclusively to mean "reverence for God." Godly people have experienced the Copernican revolution of Christian conversion from self-centeredness to God-centeredness.

How are we to train ourselves to be godly? Paul does not go into detail. But the context, and in particular the parallel between nourishment and exercise, suggest that we are to exercise ourselves in the same way that we nourish ourselves, namely, in the Word of God. Certainly it has been a long-standing Christian tradition that disciplined meditation in Scripture is indispensable to Christian health, and indeed to growth in godliness. For in contrast to "godless myths," Scripture is the most godly book that has ever been written. We cannot become familiar with this godly book without becoming godly ourselves. Nothing evokes the worship of God like the Word of God.

Paul emphasizes the importance of spiritual exercise by contrasting it with physical exercise: "physical training is of some value," since it contributes to our physical fitness in this life, "but godliness" (including the training that promotes it) "has value for all things, holding promise for both the present life and the life to come." In brief, it prepares us for eternity.

We can now bring together the two tests that Paul gave Timothy and that can still be applied to doubtful teaching today. The theological test is the doctrine of creation: does this teaching honor God as the Creator and giver of all good things? The second test is ethical and concerns the priority of godliness: does this teaching honor God by drawing out our worship? We do not need to have any hesitation about any teaching that glorifies God the Creator and promotes godliness.

A Youthful Leader

1 TIMOTHY 4:11-14

> [11]Command and teach these things. [12]Don't let anyone look down on you because you are young, but set an example for the believers in speech, in conduct, in love, in faith and in purity. [13]Until I come, devote yourself to the public reading of Scripture, to preaching and to teaching. [14]Do not neglect your gift, which was given you through prophecy when the body of elders laid their hands on you.

Timothy had been called to Christian leadership beyond his years. His responsibility to "command and teach" was in danger of being undermined by his youthfulness and by the signs that his ministry was being rejected. Paul is not concerned now with error (and how it could be detected and rejected) but with truth (and how it could be commended and so accepted).

Perhaps some people were jealous of Timothy; they resented his having been promoted over their heads. Others simply looked down their noses at this pretentious youth. Older people have always found it difficult to accept young people as responsible adults in their own right, let alone as leaders. And young people are understandably irritated when their elders keep reminding them of their immaturity and inexperience, and treat them with contempt.

How should young Christian leaders react in this situation so that their youth is not despised and their ministry is not rejected? Not by boastful, assertive, or aggressive behavior, not by throwing their weight about and trying to impose their will, but by different means altogether. The apostle offers Timothy six ways he should commend his ministry and gain acceptance for it.

First, "set an example for the believers in speech, in conduct, in love, in faith and in purity." People would not despise Timothy's youth if they could admire his example. The Christian leads by example, not force, and is to be a model who invites a following, not a boss who compels one.

Paul's next instruction is this: "Until I come, devote yourself to the public reading of Scripture, to preaching and to teaching." A certain authority had been delegated to Timothy as Paul's representative in Ephesus, but his authority was secondary, both to the Scripture and to the apostle. All Christian teachers occupy the same subordinate position as Timothy did. They will be wise, especially if they are young, to demonstrate both their submission to the authority of Scripture and their conscientious integrity in expounding it, so that their teaching is seen to be not theirs but the word of God.

Next Paul admonishes Timothy, "Do not neglect your gift, which was given you through prophecy when the body of elders laid their hands on you." It is not an anachronism to refer to this as Timothy's ordination. Timothy was young and inexperienced. But let him remember (and remind others) that God had called him (through the prophetic word), equipped him (through the heavenly gift), and commissioned him (through the elders' hands), and the people will not despise his youth or reject his teaching.

More Advice for a Youthful Leader

1 TIMOTHY 4:15-16

> [15]Be diligent in these matters; give yourself wholly to them,
> so that everyone may see your progress. [16]Watch your life
> and doctrine closely. Persevere in them, because if you do,
> you will save both yourself and your hearers.

Having referred to Timothy's example, to the biblical authority
he must teach under, and to his divine call, gift, and commissioning, Paul goes on to Timothy's need for concentration and
perseverance. "Be diligent in these matters; give yourself wholly
to them." The purpose of this commitment is "so that everyone
may see your progress." It is not only Timothy's devotion to duty
which must be seen, but his consistent spiritual growth. The
example which Christian leaders set, whether in their life or
their ministry, should be dynamic and progressive. People should
be able to observe not only what they are but what they are
becoming, supplying evidence that they are growing into maturity in Christ.

Paul next tells Timothy, "Watch your life and doctrine closely.
Persevere in them." Timothy is to keep a close eye on two things
equally: first, his *life*, literally "himself," his character and his
conduct, second, his *doctrine*, his teaching of other people. He is to
be neither so engrossed in teaching others that he neglects himself
nor so concerned with the culture of his own soul that he neglects
his ministry to others. Instead, he is to be consistent, applying
himself with equal attention and perseverance to himself and to
others. It is fatally easy to become so busy in the Lord's work that

we leave no time for the Lord himself, to be so concerned for the welfare of others that we fail to keep a watchful eye on ourselves.

"If you do" persevere in these duties, Paul concludes, "you will save both yourself and your hearers." At first sight this sentence is shocking. How could Timothy save himself? Did not Paul repeatedly insist that salvation is by grace alone in Christ alone through faith alone? Has he suddenly gone berserk and contradicted himself? No, of course not. Salvation always and everywhere originates not in us but only in the grace and mercy of God. Nevertheless, the reality of our salvation has to be demonstrated in good works of love. Perseverance is not the meritorious cause but rather the ultimate evidence, of our salvation.

And how could Timothy save his hearers? Surely only God could save them through Christ. Yes, but the New Testament not infrequently attributes salvation to evangelists, since it is through the gospel they preach that God saves believers. Neither Paul nor Timothy could save anybody. But this is dramatic language that ascribes directly to evangelists the salvation which God himself effects indirectly through the gospel they proclaim.

Older and Younger

1 TIMOTHY 5:1-2

> [1]Do not rebuke an older man harshly, but exhort him as if he were your father. Treat younger men as brothers, [2]older women as mothers, and younger women as sisters, with absolute purity.

Although a comparatively young man, Timothy found himself responsible for several congregations that were mixed both in sex (men and women) and in age (old and young). Paul now tells him that the sex and age of the people should determine his attitude to them.

Take the older people first. Paul seems to assume that it will be Timothy's duty to admonish somebody considerably older than himself. He must perform his duty, but he must do it as an exhortation, not as a harsh rebuke. Timothy is to give to senior members of the church the respect that is due to age and the affection that is due to parents.

It is true that we are all brothers and sisters in Christ. Yet it seems artificial to me in the West when students breeze up to me and call me by my first name, even though I am old enough to be their great-grandfather! The Asian and African cultures are wiser, since they encourage young people to address the older generation as "uncle" and "auntie."

Paul also advises Timothy about his attitude to people of his own generation. He is to treat younger men like "brothers," loving them and not condescending to them, and younger women like "sisters," loving them too, with sensible restraint and "absolute purity."

In brief, the local church is rightly called the church family, in which there are fathers and mothers, and brothers and sisters, not to mention aunts and uncles, grandparents and children. Leaders should not be insensitive and treat everybody alike. No, they must behave toward their elders with respect, affection, and gentleness, their own generation with equality, the opposite sex with self-control and purity, and all ages of both sexes with that love which binds together members of the same family.

There is much practical wisdom here for everybody called to Christian leadership, and especially for younger people given responsibility beyond their years. If they watch their example, becoming a model of Christlikeness; if they identify their authority, submitting to Scripture and drawing all their teaching from it; if they exercise their gift, giving evidence of God's call and of the rightness of the church's commissioning; if they show their progress, letting it be seen that their Christian life and ministry are dynamic, not static; if they mind their consistency, by practicing what they preach; and if they adjust their relationships, being sensitive to people's age and sex—then other people will not despise their youth, but will gladly and gratefully receive their ministry.

1 Timothy 4:1–5:2

....

DISCUSSION GUIDE

OPEN

What is the best advice you've ever received, and in what specific ways did it help you?

STUDY

1. What criteria for determining false teachers does Paul give in this passage?

2. The key statement in the first paragraph is that in spite of the church's role as the guardian of the truth, "some will abandon the faith." Why do people abandon their faith in God?

3. What contemporary false teachers could be described by verses 1-3?

4. Why is gratitude for what God has given us (vv. 4-5) so important in fighting false teaching?

5. From verses 6-10, what is our best defense against false teaching? Why?

6. How would you define *godliness*? It will be helpful to consider some examples of how you have seen godliness demonstrated in real life.

7. Verses 8-9 contain the third "trustworthy saying" in the pastoral letters. How does the truth of this saying help us combat false teaching?

8. Timothy had been called to Christian leadership beyond his years. His responsibility to "command and teach" (v. 11) was in danger of being undermined by his youthfulness and by the signs that his ministry was being rejected. How does Paul instruct him to live so that others will respect him?

9. When are you tempted to "neglect your gift" (v. 14)?

10. Paul told Timothy to "watch [his] life and doctrine closely." What is significant about the order of the words *life* and *doctrine*?

11. Paul gave Timothy instructions about his attitude toward those older and younger in the church. How would following Paul's guidelines build up the fellowship of a church?

APPLY

1. What specific actions are you engaged in regularly to train yourself to be godly so you won't succumb to false teaching?

5

1 Timothy 5:3–6:2
Caring for Widows

❧

Widows in Need

1 TIMOTHY 5:3-8

³Give proper recognition to those widows who are really in need. ⁴But if a widow has children or grandchildren, these should learn first of all to put their religion into practice by caring for their own family and so repaying their parents and grandparents, for this is pleasing to God. ⁵The widow who is really in need and left all alone puts her hope in God and continues night and day to pray and to ask God for help. ⁶But the widow who lives for pleasure is dead even while she lives.⁷Give the people these instructions, so that no one may be open to blame.⁸Anyone who does not provide for their relatives, and especially for their own household, has denied the faith and is worse than an unbeliever.

In Scripture widows, orphans, and aliens (people without husband, parents, or home) are valued for who they are in themselves and are said to deserve special honor, protection, and care. Throughout the Bible justice and love are demanded for them. The early church learned this lesson from the teaching of the Old Testament, as well as the example of Jesus, and continued to show the same concern.

Here the context makes it clear that the honor due to widows (their "proper recognition") must go beyond personal respect and emotional support to financial provision. But who is responsible for the financial care of widows? And which widows qualify for such support? Paul addresses these questions here, for evidently the local church was maintaining some widows who should have been supported by their own families.

The church's financial support should be limited to widows "who are really in need." Such a widow is destitute, being unable to support herself and having no dowry or relatives to support her. For "if a widow has children or grandchildren, these should learn first of all to put their religion into practice by caring for their own family." Two motives are given why family members should do this. First, it will be a way of "repaying their parents and grandparents" who cared for them when they were young. Second, it is "pleasing to God," the God who in Scripture both commands us to honor our parents and declares his own concern for widows.

Totally different from such a godly woman is "the widow who lives for pleasure," that is, for herself rather than for God. She "is dead even while she lives." For one kind of life (self-indulgence) is in reality spiritual death, while one kind of death (self-denial) is in reality spiritual life.

So there are both material and spiritual conditions of eligibility for the church's maintenance of widows. The material condition is destitution, and the spiritual condition is godliness. "Give the people these instructions," Paul continues, for the care of destitute widows is to be a church responsibility, not a personal ministry of Timothy's. Before Paul concludes this part of his instruction, however, he repeats with even stronger emphasis what he has already written about families shouldering their own responsibilities. The person who fails to provide for family "has denied the faith and is worse than an unbeliever." Strong language! But nature itself teaches that children should care for their parents, for many pagans by the light of nature have done so, and provision for widows had come to be incorporated in Roman law. Are we who have the fuller light of God's revelation to despise those whom even pagans honor?

Widows to Be Enrolled—Or Not

1 TIMOTHY 5:9-16

> [9]No widow may be put on the list of widows unless she is over sixty, has been faithful to her husband, [10]and is well known for her good deeds, such as bringing up children, showing hospitality, washing the feet of the Lord's people, helping those in trouble and devoting herself to all kinds of good deeds.
>
> [11]As for younger widows, do not put them on such a list. For when their sensual desires overcome their dedication

to Christ, they want to marry. [12]Thus they bring judgment on themselves, because they have broken their first pledge. [13]Besides, they get into the habit of being idle and going about from house to house. And not only do they become idlers, but also busybodies who talk nonsense, saying things they ought not to. [14]So I counsel younger widows to marry, to have children, to manage their homes and to give the enemy no opportunity for slander. [15]Some have in fact already turned away to follow Satan.

[16]If any woman who is a believer has widows in her care, she should continue to help them and not let the church be burdened with them, so that the church can help those widows who are really in need.

It seems that this "list of widows" is not for widows needing support but for widows capable of offering service. Paul lists the three qualifications for registration: seniority, married fidelity, and good works.

The first qualification to be registered is that she should be "over sixty" and therefore unlikely to wish to remarry. Second, she must have been "faithful to her husband." Third, a widow must be "well known for her good deeds." Paul enumerates a number of those commendable actions. Such a record of humble, unselfish, and costly service would qualify a registered widow to undertake similar ministries as an accredited church worker.

It is clear that younger widows would not qualify to be enrolled. So Paul gives Timothy a different set of instructions for them, for two reasons. The first is that younger women would become restive in their single state and would naturally want to remarry. Their natural desires would become stronger than their commitment to stay single and serve the church.

The second reason for not registering younger widows is uncertainty whether they will be able to concentrate on responsible service. Therefore Paul counsels the younger widows to marry. Although the apostle expressed a personal preference for singleness, he acknowledged that each person has his or her own grace gift from God, whether to marry or not to marry. He recognizes that single people are free to become engrossed in the affairs of the Lord, while married people tend to become preoccupied with the affairs of the world.

Two lasting principles of social welfare seem to emerge from these apostolic instructions. The first is the principle of discernment. There was to be no general handout to all widows regardless of their circumstances. The church's welfare provisions are to be limited to those in genuine need. If there are any alternative means of support, they should be used. In particular, the first call is on the family. The church's sense of social responsibility is not to encourage irresponsibility in others.

Second, there is the principle of dignity. Ideally, health and strength permitting, the supported widows and the serving widows should be the same people. Widows (together with others in similar circumstances) should have the opportunity both to receive according to their need and to give according to their ability, that is, both to be served and to serve. Christian relief should never demean its beneficiaries, but rather should increase their sense of dignity.

Honoring Elders

1 TIMOTHY 5:17-18

> [17]The elders who direct the affairs of the church well are worthy of double honor, especially those whose work is preaching and teaching. [18]For Scripture says, "Do not muzzle an ox while it is treading out the grain," and "The worker deserves his wages."

We sometimes say or think that Christian workers need the appreciation only of the Chief Shepherd and not of human leaders. Paul was of a different opinion. Human beings are prone to discouragement and need to be affirmed. So elders who do "well" in their work "are worthy of double honor."

What kind of honor does Paul have in mind? From the quotations of the following verse, it is clear that it includes adequate remuneration. Yet it seems unlikely that Paul is referring only to pay. Conscientious elders should receive both respect and remuneration, both honor and an honorarium. Paul took it for granted that the pastorate was a paid ministry. As in Old Testament days the priests were supported in order to devote themselves to the Lord's service, so in New Testament days pastors should be supported so that they can devote themselves to the work of the gospel.

The apostle provides biblical authority for what he is saying by bringing together two quotations. The first is from Deuteronomy 25:4: "Do not muzzle an ox while it is treading out the grain." If God is concerned that working animals are adequately fed, how much more concern must he have for church workers?

Paul's second quotation follows: "The worker deserves his wages." Although Paul does not attribute these words to Jesus, they do occur in Luke 10:7.

Paul's purpose in employing these models is to emphasize that the elders' service is hard work, and hard work performed conscientiously deserves to be rewarded. Good work is to be appreciated, and appreciation may quite properly take a tangible financial form.

Accusations Against Elders

1 TIMOTHY 5:19-21

> [19]Do not entertain an accusation against an elder unless it is brought by two or three witnesses. [20]But those elders who are sinning you are to reprove before everyone, so that the others may take warning. [21]I charge you, in the sight of God and Christ Jesus and the elect angels, to keep these instructions without partiality, and to do nothing out of favoritism.

Paul now turns from good pastors who deserve appreciation to bad ones who may deserve a rebuke. The situation envisioned is one in which a complaint or accusation is made to Timothy about an elder. Paul gives him two complementary directions, first when an elder is accused of something, and second when the elder is found guilty.

First, an accusation must be substantiated by several people. In the Old Testament two or three witnesses were required to sustain a charge and secure a conviction, especially in regard to a capital charge. The same principle applies in New Testament times, in particular when Christian leaders are being accused. Indeed, two or three witnesses are required not only before an accusation is sustained, but before it is entertained at all.

This practical regulation is necessary for the protection of pastoral leaders, who are vulnerable to slander. A smear campaign can completely ruin a leader's ministry. So Paul's first word to Timothy is that he must never listen to gossip about leaders or even to a serious accusation if it is made by only one person. Every charge must be endorsed by several responsible people before it is even listened to. Adherence to this biblical principle would silence many a malicious talebearer and save many pastors from unjust criticism and unnecessary suffering.

Second, if an accusation against an elder is not only confirmed by two or three witnesses but is proved, and if the elder concerned, though admonished privately, refuses to repent but persists in sin, then the sadness and the scandal of a public showdown cannot be avoided. Such a public rebuke, though an effective deterrent, must be the last resort. It is neither right nor necessary to make what is private public until all other possibilities have been exhausted.

In short, Timothy must neither listen to frivolous accusations nor refuse to take serious situations seriously.

Paul now issues a charge to Timothy couched in the most solemn terms. Two negatives are emphasized. The first is to act "without partiality," without jumping to conclusions of either guilt or innocence. The second negative injunction is "to do nothing out of favoritism." Christian leaders should show no special treatment to those of their own clan, to members of their own class or tribe, to people they happen to like, or to those to whom for some reason they are indebted. Paul charges Timothy "to keep these instructions," namely, the principles governing the treatment of elders, and to do so with absolute fairness and without any taint of injustice.

Caution and Discernment

I TIMOTHY 5:22-25

²²Do not be hasty in the laying on of hands, and do not share in the sins of others. Keep yourself pure.

²³Stop drinking only water, and use a little wine because of your stomach and your frequent illnesses.

²⁴The sins of some are obvious, reaching the place of judgment ahead of them; the sins of others trail behind them. ²⁵In the same way, good deeds are obvious, and even those that are not obvious cannot remain hidden forever.

It is a common human tendency to make premature and ill-considered decisions, to be hasty when we should rather be cautious. Although the opposite fault is to be indecisive, yet in leaders it is better to take time to form judgments and make decisions than to be incautious and live to regret it. So Paul bids Timothy: "Do not be hasty in the laying on of hands." It is most likely that Paul is referring to ordination. In verse 20 Paul mentioned the possible need to publicly rebuke an elder. The best way to avoid such a scandal is to ensure the thorough screening of candidates before they are ordained. Otherwise, if through excessive haste a mistake is made and a scandal arises, Timothy will "share in the sins of others."

Verse 23, in which the apostle exhorts Timothy to "stop drinking only water" and to "use a little wine because of your stomach and your frequent illnesses," has no obvious connection with what precedes or follows. Some think that Paul's injunction to "keep yourself pure" reminded him to add "keep yourself fit" as well. Wine was widely recognized in the ancient world as having medicinal properties, and Paul was perhaps anxious that Timothy was not looking after himself properly.

Verses 24 and 25 develop Paul's emphasis on the need for caution and give a further reason to avoid haste. It is that human beings are frequently different from what they appear at first sight. They may seem initially either better or worse than they really are, for both their good and their bad points may take a while to surface. Therefore time is needed in which to discover the truth about a candidate for the pastorate. So Timothy would need discernment. Attractive personalities often have hidden weaknesses, whereas unprepossessing people often have hidden strengths. Timothy must learn to discern between the seen and the unseen, the surface and the depth, the appearance and the reality.

If Timothy follows the leadership principles Paul has laid down, mistakes will be avoided, the church will be preserved in peace and love, and God's name will be protected from dishonor.

Believing Slaves

1 TIMOTHY 6:1-2

[1]All who are under the yoke of slavery should consider their masters worthy of full respect, so that God's name and our

teaching may not be slandered. ²Those who have believing masters should not show them disrespect just because they are fellow believers. Instead, they should serve them even better because their masters are dear to them as fellow believers and are devoted to the welfare of their slaves.

These are the things you are to teach and insist on.

There is nothing demeaning about service when it is given voluntarily. What is degrading and fundamentally destructive of a person's humanness is when one human being is forcibly owned by another and is thus robbed of all freedom. Even though some slave owners in the Roman Empire were kind to their slaves since they saw them as a valuable investment, the institution itself was a denial of human personhood.

Why is it, then, that neither Jesus nor his apostles called for the complete and immediate abolition of this horror? Probably the main reason is that slavery was deeply embedded in the structures of Greco-Roman society. Slaves were regarded as essential, especially as domestic servants and farm laborers, but also as clerks, craftsmen, teachers, soldiers, and managers. To dismantle slavery all at once would have brought about the collapse of society. At the same time Paul enunciated principles that undermined the very concept of slavery and led inexorably to its abolition, even though Christians are ashamed that it did not happen sooner.

In verses 1 and 2, the slaves Timothy is to instruct are clearly Christians and church members. But whereas in verse 2 we are explicitly told that the slave owner is a believer, in verse 1 it seems likely that the owner is not. So Timothy is to adjust his teaching to the context.

First, slaves "should consider their masters," even though they are unbelievers, to be "worthy of full respect." That is, they will treat them with respect because they are human beings, irrespective of their behavior. Then there is a missionary reason why slaves should respect their masters. It is because the reputation of "God's name and our teaching" (meaning that of the apostles) is at stake. If slaves show disrespect for their masters, they will bring discredit on God's name and the apostles' teaching; however, these will "not be slandered," but will rather be honored, if they respect their masters.

Second, "those who have believing masters should not show them disrespect just because they are fellow believers." Evidently some slaves were guilty of this twisted reasoning and were taking advantage of their masters' Christian faith. On the contrary, because their masters are fellow believers, slaves "should serve them even better." The faith, love, and family relationship that unite them in Christ, far from being an excuse for neglect, should be a stimulus to service.

1 Timothy 5:3–6:2

....

Discussion Guide

Open

How do you feel when you know someone respects you? How about when someone doesn't respect you?

Study

1. What qualifies a widow as one "in need" and thus deserving of support by the church?

2. How can we give "proper recognition" to widows (and people in similar circumstances) in the church today?

3. How is taking care of one's family, including widows who are part of it, a testimony to others?

4. According to verse 9, the early church had a register or list of widows. Consider the qualifications for being on that list. Why is each important?

5. What general principles do the steps and qualifications outlined here teach us about offering care to people in need?

6. In verses 17-18, how does Paul reinforce his point of appreciating elders?

7. According to verses 19-20, how should a church handle accusations against an elder? (See also Deuteronomy 19:15.)

8. What will this procedure do to potential gossip?

9. In verse 21, what dangers did Paul warn Timothy about, and why?

10. What impact do both sins and good deeds have on others?

11. How should Christian employees view their Christian and non-Christian employers, and why?

12. How does the theme of honoring others run throughout this entire Scripture passage?

APPLY

1. In what situations do you need to show more respect for others, regardless of your position relative to each other?

6

1 Timothy 6:3-21
Money Matters

❦

Troublemaking Teachers

1 TIMOTHY 6:3-5

³If anyone teaches otherwise and does not agree to the sound instruction of our Lord Jesus Christ and to godly teaching, ⁴they are conceited and understand nothing. They have an unhealthy interest in controversies and quarrels about words that result in envy, strife, malicious talk, evil suspicions ⁵and constant friction between people of corrupt mind, who have been robbed of the truth and who think that godliness is a means to financial gain.

Having given Timothy instructions about three groups in the church (widows, elders, and slaves), Paul comes to a fourth (false teachers), whose poisonous influence is at the back of his mind throughout this letter. The apostle evaluates the false teachers in relation to questions of truth, unity, and motivation. His criticism of them is that they deviate from the faith, split the church, and love money.

Once again Paul implies that there is a standard of Christian belief, which he calls "the sound instruction of our Lord Jesus Christ" and "godly teaching." So here are two essential marks of sound teaching: it comes from Christ, and it promotes godliness. From this norm the false teachers have turned aside.

In addition to being arrogant and ignorant, the false teachers are divisive. It is noteworthy that Paul portrays their interest in controversy as "unhealthy," while the apostolic teaching is "sound" or healthy. The false teachers' relish for profitless argument is pathological.

Petty quibbles and quarrels of this kind lead to a complete breakdown in human relationships. Five results are listed: "envy" (the resentment of other people's gifts), "strife" (the spirit of competition and contention), "malicious talk" (verbal abuse of others), "evil suspicions" (forgetting that fellowship is built on trust), and "constant friction" (the fruit of irritability). These evils characterize "people of corrupt mind." When people's minds are twisted, all their relationships become twisted too.

Another symptom of the false teachers' depraved mind and loss of truth is that they "think that godliness is a means to financial gain." They have no interest in godliness itself, but only if it proves to be financially profitable. Precisely how the false teachers Timothy had to combat were exploiting godliness for gain is not divulged. But we do know that Ephesus enjoyed great opulence, inflated by the trade that the cult of Diana brought to the city. The history of the human race has regularly been stained by attempts to commercialize religion.

Looking back over verses 3-5, we note that Paul has given us three practical tests by which to evaluate all teaching. Is it compatible with the apostolic faith, that is, the New Testament? Does it tend to unite or to divide the church? And does it promote godliness with contentment, or covetousness?

The Christian Poor

1 TIMOTHY 6:6-10

> [6]But godliness with contentment is great gain. [7]For we brought nothing into the world, and we can take nothing out of it. [8]But if we have food and clothing, we will be content with that. [9]Those who want to get rich fall into temptation and a trap and into many foolish and harmful desires that plunge people into ruin and destruction. [10]For the love of money is a root of all kinds of evil. Some people, eager for money, have wandered from the faith and pierced themselves with many griefs.

Our life on earth is a brief pilgrimage between two moments of nakedness. Possessions are only the traveling luggage of time; they are not the stuff of eternity.

Then what should be our attitude to material things? Paul replies: "if we have food and clothing, we will be content with that." Probably "food and clothing" should be extended to include shelter, for these three are clearly essential for our journey. What Paul is defining is not the maximum that is permitted to the believer but the minimum that is compatible with contentment. He is not advocating austerity or asceticism, but contentment in place of materialism and covetousness.

Paul now traces the downfall of the covetous. They "fall into temptation and a trap." They do to themselves what they pray God will never do to them: they lead themselves into temptation, indeed into multiple temptations like dishonesty and theft. They fall "into many foolish and harmful desires." Of course greed is itself a desire, but it breeds other desires. These further desires are "foolish and harmful," and they "plunge people into ruin and destruction." The metaphor pictures them sinking and drowning. The irony is that those who set their hearts on gain end in total loss: the loss of their integrity and indeed of themselves.

In order to enforce his solemn warning, Paul quotes what seems to have been a current proverb: "For the love of money is a root of all kinds of evil." This is often misquoted as "Money is the root of all evil," but according to Paul the problem is not money but "the love of money." It is not the one and only root of evil, but it is "a root." And it is not the root of "all evil" in the singular, but a root of "all kinds of evil" in the plural.

What are the evils of which the love of money is a major root or cause? A long list could be given. Paul concentrates on only two. First, some "have wandered from the faith." People either renounce greed in their commitment to the faith, or they make money their god and depart from the faith. Second, they have "pierced themselves with many griefs." These griefs are not identified, but they could include worry and remorse, the pangs of a disregarded conscience, the discovery that materialism can never satisfy the human spirit, and finally despair.

The apostle's essential emphasis is clear, namely, that covetousness is a self-destructive evil, whereas simplicity and contentment are beautiful and Christlike virtues. In a word, he is not for poverty against wealth, but for contentment against covetousness.

Fight the Good Fight

1 TIMOTHY 6:11-12

> [11]But you, man of God, flee from all this, and pursue righteousness, godliness, faith, love, endurance and gentleness. [12]Fight the good fight of the faith. Take hold of the eternal life to which you were called when you made your good confession in the presence of many witnesses.

As a "man of God," Timothy is to be radically different from the divisive and money-hungry false teachers. He must take a firm stand against their ungodliness. Paul develops a threefold appeal to him—ethical, doctrinal, and experiential.

The ethical appeal. As a man of God, Timothy must both "flee from all this" (the love of money and its associated evils) and "pursue" six qualities that are particularly appropriate as an alternative to covetousness. Negatively, we are to "flee from" evil, to run from it as far as we can and as fast as we can. Positively, we are to "pursue" goodness, to go in hot pursuit of it.

To run from a real danger is common sense, but to run from issues we dare not face or from responsibilities we dare not shoulder is escapism. Instead, we should concentrate on running away from evil. We also run after many things that attract us—pleasure, promotion, fame, wealth, and power. Instead, we should concentrate on the pursuit of holiness.

The doctrinal appeal. "Fight the good fight of the faith." Timothy's duty will involve fight as well as flight, standing as well as running. Fighting is an unpleasant business—undignified, bloody, painful, and dangerous. So is controversy, that is, fighting for truth and goodness. It should be distasteful to all sensitive spirits. Nevertheless, this is a "good fight"; it has to be fought. For God's truth is precious, even sacred. It is essential for the health and growth of the church. Whenever truth is imperiled by false teachers, to defend it is a painful necessity.

The experiential appeal. "Take hold of . . . eternal life." Eternal life means the life of the age to come, the new age Jesus inaugurated. It may seem strange that a Christian leader of Timothy's stature should need to be exhorted to "take hold of" eternal life. Why did Paul tell him to lay hold of what he already possessed? The probable answer is that it is possible to possess something without embracing and enjoying it. Although Timothy had already received eternal life, Paul urged him to seize it, grasp it, lay hold of it, make it completely his own, enjoy it, and live it to the full.

It is good in our relativistic age to have truth, goodness, and life set before us as absolute goals. They also constitute a healthy balance. Some fight for truth but neglect holiness. Others pursue holiness but have no comparable concern for truth. Still others disregard both doctrine and ethics in their search for religious experience. The man or woman of God combines all three.

In the Sight of God

1 TIMOTHY 6:13-16

> [13]In the sight of God, who gives life to everything, and of Christ Jesus, who while testifying before Pontius Pilate made the good confession, I charge you [14]to keep this command without spot or blame until the appearing of our Lord Jesus Christ, [15]which God will bring about in his own time—God, the blessed and only Ruler, the King of kings and Lord of lords, [16]who alone is immortal and who lives in unapproachable light, whom no one has seen or can see. To him be honor and might forever. Amen.

Paul does more than appeal to Timothy, for he knows about human apathy and our consequent need for incentives. So he buttresses his appeal with strong arguments, namely, the presence of God and the coming of Christ.

First, Paul lived so much in the conscious presence of God that it was natural for him to write: "In the sight of God . . . and of Christ Jesus . . . I charge you." Moreover, he reminds himself and Timothy of an appropriate truth about each. He describes God as the one "who gives life to everything." As the giver and sustainer of the life of all living creatures, God is intimately involved in their affairs. Christ, on the other hand, is described as the one "who while testifying before Pontius Pilate made the good confession" by acknowledging that he was indeed a king. Jesus' disciples never forgot the historical precedent of bold testimony that he set.

The second ground on which the apostle bases his charge is the second coming of Christ. Paul is as certain about the event as he is uncertain about its time. Yet he knows that this too is in God's hands, since he "will bring *it* about in his own time." This assurance about the divine timetable is a notable feature of Paul's pastoral letters.

Our confidence in God's perfect timing and our consequent willingness to leave things in his hands arise from the kind of God we know him to be. This Paul goes on to unfold, probably drawing on the words of an early Christian hymn. He affirms four truths about God's sovereign power.

First, God is invincible, beyond all interference by earthly powers. No human rule can challenge his authority.

Second, God is immortal, not subject to changes caused by time, death, or dissolution. Human beings also are immortal in the sense that we survive death, but only God has life in himself.

Third, God is inaccessible, beyond the reach of sinful people. Darkness in any shape or form, whether falsehood or evil, cannot enter his presence, let alone overcome him.

Fourth, God is invisible, beyond human sight and human apprehension. We can come to know him only insofar as he has been pleased to make himself known. Otherwise, he is wholly beyond us.

When he writes about God, Paul naturally breaks into a doxology: to this great God, invincible, immortal, inaccessible, and invisible, "be honor and might for ever. Amen." In the presence of this God, and in anticipation of his bringing about Christ's appearing, Paul has given Timothy his solemn charge. Still today the presence of God and the appearing of Christ are two major incentives to faithfulness.

The Christian Rich

1 TIMOTHY 6:17-19

[17]Command those who are rich in this present world not to be arrogant nor to put their hope in wealth, which is so uncertain, but to put their hope in God, who richly provides us with everything for our enjoyment. [18]Command them to do good, to be rich in good deeds, and to be generous and willing to share. [19]In this way they will lay up treasure for themselves as a firm foundation for the coming age, so that they may take hold of the life that is truly life.

Wealth and poverty are relative terms. Neither can be neatly defined. Among the poor some are poorer than others, and among the wealthy some are wealthier than others. Nevertheless, in every culture there is a recognized difference between them.

Notice that Paul does not direct the rich to divest themselves of their riches. Instead, he gives negative and positive instruction, first warning the rich of the dangers of wealth, then laying down their obligations.

The first danger to which the wealthy are exposed is pride. The Old Testament clearly warned people of this. Wealth often gives birth to vanity and makes people feel self-important.

The second danger to which the rich are exposed is a false security. The proper object of our human trust is not a thing but a Person, not uncertain wealth but *God*, "who richly provides us with everything for our enjoyment." God is our generous Creator who wants us to appreciate the good gifts of creation. If we consider it right to adopt an economic lifestyle lower than we could command, it will be out of solidarity with the poor, not because we judge the possession of material things to be wrong in itself.

The two dangers, then, to which the rich are exposed are false pride (looking down on people less fortunate than themselves) and false security (trusting in the gift instead of in the Giver). In this way wealth can spoil life's two paramount relationships, causing us to forget God and despise our neighbor.

Timothy is not only to warn the rich of the perils they face, but also to alert them to the duties they have.

First, Timothy must seek to develop in the rich a sense of responsibility. Let them add one kind of wealth to another by being "rich in good deeds." Wealth can make people lazy. Since God is such a generous giver, his people should be generous too, not only in imitation of his generosity but also because of the colossal needs of the world around us.

Second, Timothy must seek to develop in the rich a sense of proportion. The "treasure for themselves" that the wealthy lay up by their generosity is clearly not material treasure but spiritual treasure, enabling the generous rich to lay hold of the authentic life that begins now and ends in heaven.

Bringing together Paul's negative and positive instructions to the wealthy, they are not to be proud and despise the poor, but to do good and be generous; they are not to fix their hopes on uncertain riches but on God the Giver and on that most valuable of all his gifts, the treasure of eternal life.

Guard the Faith

1 TIMOTHY 6:20-21

²⁰Timothy, guard what has been entrusted to your care. Turn away from godless chatter and the opposing ideas of what is falsely called knowledge, ²¹which some have professed and in so doing have departed from the faith.

Grace be with you all.

In his final personal charge to Timothy, Paul reverts to the false teachers whose damaging activity has been the background of the whole letter. He contrasts two sets of teaching (his and theirs) and two possible attitudes (guarding the former and turning away from the latter).

Paul calls his own teaching "what has been entrusted to your care," literally a deposit of money or valuables left with somebody for safekeeping. Here the deposit is "the faith." Timothy is to "guard" it, preserving it and passing it on to others without dilution or distortion.

The false teaching, on the other hand, Paul urges Timothy to "turn away from" or avoid. Paul adds that those who "have professed" these ideas "have departed from the faith," that is, from the teaching of the apostles.

Paul's concluding prayer, "Grace be with you all," indicates that Paul is looking beyond Timothy, as he has done throughout the letter, to the congregations he is supervising. They would not be able in their own strength to reject error and fight for truth, to run from evil and pursue goodness, to renounce covetousness and cultivate contentment and generosity, and in these Christian responsibilities to remain faithful to the end. Only divine grace could keep them. So at the letter's conclusion, as at its beginning, the apostle wishes for them above all else an experience of the transforming and sustaining grace of God.

1 Timothy 6:3-21

....

Discussion Guide

Open

What evidences of the love of money do you see among Christians today (both those who have money and those who lack it)?

Study

1. In contrast to "sound instruction," what characteristics and motives of false teachers did Paul focus on in verses 3-5?

2. What are the results of their false teachings?

3. How is godliness with contentment "great gain" (v. 6)?

4. How does Paul argue for contentment and against greed?

5. What should be a Christian's attitude toward material possessions?

6. What is the price people pay for their love of money?

7. What did Paul tell Timothy to do to combat covetousness (vv. 11-16)? Give an example of each action.

8. What do you learn about God from Paul's supporting arguments for Timothy to "keep this command" (v. 14)?

9. After a digression (vv. 11-16), Paul reverts to the topic of money in verses 17-19. What are the dangers of being rich?

10. What obligations come with having wealth?

11. Consider Paul's final charge to Timothy (vv. 20-21). Why do you think he ended his letter that way?

APPLY

1. What practical steps can you take to flee materialism and follow godliness?

2. How can you use the resources God has given you—whatever the amount—to do good works?

2 Timothy 1
Stand Up for the Gospel

❦

From Apostle to Dear Son

2 TIMOTHY 1:1-2

> ¹Paul, an apostle of Christ Jesus by the will of God, in keeping with the promise of life that is in Christ Jesus,
>
> ²To Timothy, my dear son:
>
> Grace, mercy and peace from God the Father and Christ Jesus our Lord.

In styling himself "an apostle of Christ Jesus," Paul is advancing a considerable claim for himself. He ranks himself with the Twelve Jesus personally selected out of the wider company of his disciples. Even at the moment of writing, humiliated by people and awaiting the emperor's pleasure, this common prisoner is a privileged apostle of Christ Jesus, the King of kings.

Paul goes on to describe his apostleship in two ways. He reminds Timothy of both its origin and its object.

Its origin was "the will of God." Paul's sustained conviction, from the beginning to the end of his apostolic career, was that his appointment as an apostle had come neither from the church nor from any person or group of people; nor was he self-appointed. On the contrary, his apostleship originated in the eternal will and historical call of almighty God through Jesus Christ.

The object of Paul's apostleship concerns "the promise of life that is in Christ Jesus." He had been commissioned as an apostle first to formulate and then to communicate the gospel. And the gospel is good news for dying sinners that God has promised them life in Jesus Christ. It is particularly appropriate that, as death stares the apostle in the face, he should define it here as a "promise of life." The gospel does more than offer life; it promises life to all who are in Christ.

Paul calls Timothy "my dear son" presumably because he had been the human instrument of Timothy's conversion. To his spiritual son, Paul now sends his greeting of "grace, mercy and peace." This threefold greeting is no mere convention, for these are heavily charged theological words. They tell us much about humanity's sorry condition in sin and about God's great love for us all the same. For if "grace" is God's kindness to the undeserving, "mercy" is shown to the weak and helpless who cannot help themselves. "Mercy" converted Saul of Tarsus, the confirmed blasphemer and persecutor. "Peace," on the other hand, is reconciliation, the restoration of harmony to lives spoiled by discord.

We may summarize these three blessings of God's love as being *grace* to the undeserving, *mercy* to the helpless, and *peace* to the restless, while "God the Father and Christ Jesus our Lord" together constitute the one spring from which this threefold stream flows forth.

Parents, Grandparents, Friends

2 TIMOTHY 1:3-5

> [3]I thank God, whom I serve, as my ancestors did, with a clear conscience, as night and day I constantly remember you in my prayers. [4]Recalling your tears, I long to see you, so that I may be filled with joy. [5]I am reminded of your sincere faith, which first lived in your grandmother Lois and in your mother Eunice and, I am persuaded, now lives in you also.

Now comes a very personal paragraph in which the apostle assures Timothy that he constantly remembers him, and that whenever he does, he thanks God. This is significant, for it indicates Paul's recognition that it was God who had made Timothy what he was. Timothy was not an apostle like Paul, but he was a Christian minister, a missionary, and an apostolic delegate. God had been at work in his life to make him all these things.

Paul refers in this paragraph both to his own and to Timothy's ancestry. This was right, for each of us is to a great extent the product of our parentage and our home.

Timothy had been raised in a godly home. His father was Greek and his mother Jewish (Acts 16:1). Presumably his

father was an unbeliever, but his mother Eunice was a believing Jew who became a Christian. Before her, his grandmother Lois had evidently been converted, for Paul writes of
the "sincere faith" of all three generations. Perhaps grandmother, mother, and son all owed their conversion to Paul
when he brought the gospel to Lystra. Even before their conversion to Christ, however, these godly Jewish women had
instructed Timothy out of the Old Testament, for Paul writes
later that Timothy has known the Scriptures "from infancy"
(2 Timothy 3:15).

Paul could say much the same of himself. He was serving
God "with a clear conscience" as his ancestors had done before
him. Of course his faith became richer, fuller, and deeper when
God revealed Christ to him. Yet it was still substantially the
same faith as that of Old Testament believers like Abraham and
David, for it was the same God they had all believed in.

After our parents, it is our friends who influence us most,
especially if they are also in some sense our teachers. Timothy
had in Paul an outstanding teacher friend. We have already seen
that Paul was Timothy's spiritual father. Having led him to
Christ, however, he did not abandon or forget him. He constantly remembered him, as he says repeatedly in this passage.
He had also taken him with him on his journeys and trained
him as his apprentice. Such a Christian friendship, including the
companionship, the letters, and the prayers it was expressed
through, did not fail to have a powerful molding effect on young
Timothy, strengthening and sustaining him in his Christian life
and service.

Rekindle the Gift

2 TIMOTHY 1:6-8

> [6]For this reason I remind you to fan into flame the gift of God, which is in you through the laying on of my hands. [7]For the Spirit God gave us does not make us timid, but gives us power, love and self-discipline. [8]So do not be ashamed of the testimony about our Lord or of me his prisoner. Rather, join with me in suffering for the gospel, by the power of God.

Paul turns from the indirect means God used to shape Timothy's Christian character (his parents and friends) to a direct gift God had given him. What this gift of God's grace was, this "charisma," we are not told. What is clear from this verse and from a similar reference in 1 Timothy 4:14 is that the gift was bestowed on him when Paul and certain elders (probably of the Lystra church) laid their hands on him. This seems to refer to Timothy's ordination or commissioning. If this is correct, then the gift was related to Timothy's ministry of the gospel. It included both the office and the spiritual equipment needed to fulfill it.

All God's gifts—natural and spiritual—need to be developed and used. Paul has already told Timothy "Do not neglect your gift" (1 Timothy 4:14), and here he urges Timothy to "fan into flame the gift of God," to *kindle* or *rekindle* it. Paul's exhortation is to continue fanning it, to keep it alive, presumably by exercising the gift faithfully and by waiting on God in prayer for its constant renewal.

Paul immediately adds his reason: "for the Spirit God gave us does not make us timid, but gives us power, love and self-discipline." Timothy was apparently a shy and sensitive person to whom responsibility was an onerous burden. Perhaps he was also fearful of spiritual excesses and extravagances. So Paul is obliged not only to urge him to keep stirring up his gift, but to reassure him that he need not shrink from exercising it.

Paul now turns from the factors that had contributed to the making of Timothy to the truth of the gospel and to Timothy's responsibility in relation to the gospel. He begs Timothy not to be "ashamed of the testimony." Suffering rather than shame is to characterize Timothy's ministry. He may be young, frail, timid, and weak. He may shrink from the tasks he is being called to. But God has molded and gifted him for his ministry. He must not be ashamed or afraid to exercise it.

If Timothy must not be ashamed of the Lord, he must not be ashamed of Paul either. When Paul was rearrested and put in chains, nearly all his former supporters forsook him. He begs Timothy not to follow suit. Paul may be the emperor's prisoner in the eyes of others; he is the Lord's prisoner in reality, his willing captive, held in prison only by Christ's permission and for Christ's sake.

God's Purpose and Grace

2 TIMOTHY 1:9-10

> [9]He has saved us and called us to a holy life—not because of anything we have done but because of his own purpose

and grace. This grace was given us in Christ Jesus before the beginning of time, [10]but it has now been revealed through the appearing of our Savior, Christ Jesus, who has destroyed death and has brought life and immortality to light through the gospel.

When God calls us to himself, he calls us to "a holy life." But if holiness is an integral part of God's plan of salvation, so is the "immortality" Paul writes of. Indeed forgiveness, holiness, and immortality are all three aspects of God's great salvation. The term *salvation* urgently needs to be rescued from the meager concepts to which we tend to degrade it. *Salvation* is a majestic word, denoting that comprehensive purpose of God by which he justifies, sanctifies, and glorifies his people.

Where does such a great salvation come from? From the "grace . . . given us in Christ Jesus before the beginning of time." If we want to trace the river of salvation to its source, we must look back beyond time to a past eternity. God gave us his own purpose of grace in Christ before we did any good works, before we were born and could do any good works, indeed before history, before time, in eternity.

Our salvation rests firmly grounded on the historical work performed by Jesus Christ at his first appearing. For though God gave us his grace in Christ Jesus "before the beginning of time," he "revealed" it in time, "now," through the appearing of the same Christ Jesus our Savior. Both divine stages were in and through Jesus Christ, but the giving was eternal and secret, while the manifesting was historical and public.

What did Christ do when he appeared and proceeded to manifest God's eternal purpose of grace? First, he "destroyed death." This cannot mean that he eliminated it, as we know from our everyday experience. But for Christian believers, death is no longer the monster it once seemed to us and still seems to many. Physical death is simply falling asleep in Christ. And spiritual death has given place to that eternal life which is communion with God begun on earth and perfected in heaven. Second, Christ "brought life and immortality to light through the gospel." This is the positive counterpart. It is by his death and resurrection that Christ destroyed death; it is through the gospel that he now reveals what he has done and offers us the life and immortality he has won for us.

Who is this that writes so confidently about the abolition of death and the revelation of life? It is Paul, who is facing the prospect of imminent death himself. Any day now he expects to receive the death sentence. Already the final summons is ringing in his ears. Yet in the very presence of death, he can shout aloud that "Christ . . . has destroyed death." This is Christian faith triumphant!

He Is Able

2 TIMOTHY 1:11-12

> [11]And of this gospel I was appointed a herald and an apostle and a teacher. [12]That is why I am suffering as I am. Yet this is no cause for shame, because I know whom I have believed, and am convinced that he is able to guard what I have entrusted to him until that day.

Although there are no apostles of Christ today, there are certainly heralds and teachers, men and women called by God to devote themselves to the work of preaching and teaching. While only some are specifically called to the ministry of preaching and teaching, every Christian believer is to be a witness and to testify to Jesus Christ out of their own personal experience.

Paul has already summoned Timothy not to be ashamed but to take his share of suffering for the gospel, and he will enlarge on this theme later in his letter. But now he emphasizes that he is not asking from Timothy something he is not prepared to experience himself. "That is why I am suffering as I am."

What is there about the gospel that people hate and oppose, and on account of which those who preach it have to suffer? It is that God saves sinners in virtue of his own purpose and grace, and not in virtue of their good works. It is the undeserved freeness of the gospel that offends. Natural or unregenerate humanity hates to have to admit the gravity of their sin and guilt, their complete helplessness to save themselves, the indispensable necessity of God's grace and Christ's sin-bearing death to save them, and therefore their inescapable indebtedness to the cross. Many preachers succumb to the temptation to mute the offense of the cross. They substitute human merit for Christ and his cross in order to avoid opposition. But no one can preach Christ crucified with faithfulness and escape opposition, even persecution.

The words "what I have entrusted to him" are a rendering of "my deposit." Both the verb *guard* and the noun *deposit* are precisely the same here in verse 12 as in verse 14 and in 1 Timothy 6:20, where they refer to the gospel. The presumption is therefore that "my deposit" is not what I have committed to Christ, but what he has committed to me. The deposit is "mine," Paul could say, because Christ had committed it to him. Yet Paul was persuaded that Christ would himself keep it safe "until that day" when Paul would have to give an account of his stewardship.

What was the ground of his confidence? "I know whom I have believed." Paul knew Christ in whom he had put his trust and was convinced of his ability to keep the deposit safe. Paul could say, "He has entrusted it to me, but he will take care of it himself." And now that Paul is entrusting it to Timothy, Timothy can be sustained by the same assurance.

Guard the Gospel

2 TIMOTHY 1:13-18

> [13]What you heard from me, keep as the pattern of sound teaching, with faith and love in Christ Jesus. [14]Guard the good deposit that was entrusted to you—guard it with the help of the Holy Spirit who lives in us.
>
> [15]You know that everyone in the province of Asia has deserted me, including Phygelus and Hermogenes.
>
> [16]May the Lord show mercy to the household of Onesiphorus, because he often refreshed me and was not ashamed of my chains. [17]On the contrary, when he was in Rome, he searched hard for me until he found me. [18]May the Lord grant that he will find mercy from the Lord on that day! You know very well in how many ways he helped me in Ephesus.

Paul's "sound teaching" is to be Timothy's guide or rule. He is not to depart from it. He is to follow it, better to hold it fast. And he must do so "with faith and love in Christ Jesus." Paul is concerned not just with what Timothy is to do but with how he does it. His personal doctrinal convictions and his instruction of others are to be characterized by faith and love.

The apostolic faith is not only "the pattern of sound teaching"; it is also "the good deposit." The gospel is a treasure deposited for safekeeping with the church. Christ had entrusted it to Paul, and Paul now entrusts it to Timothy.

Timothy must "guard" the gospel all the more tenaciously because of what had happened in and around Ephesus. There were heretics abroad, bent on corrupting the gospel and so robbing the church of the priceless treasure that had been entrusted to it. We know nothing of Phygelus and Hermogenes, but their mention suggests they were the ringleaders of a general repudiation of Paul. In any case, Paul saw the turning away of the Asian churches as more than a personal desertion; it was a disavowal of his apostolic authority.

The one bright exception appears to have been Onesiphorus, who had often offered Paul hospitality and had rendered him other, unspecified service in Ephesus. He was not ashamed of Paul's chains, which seems to mean both that he did not repudiate him at the time of his arrest and that he then followed him, even accompanied him, to Rome. Paul had good reason to be grateful for this faithful and courageous friend.

To guard the gospel in such a situation of almost universal apostasy would be a heavy responsibility for anyone, let alone a young man of Timothy's temperament. How could he stand firm? The apostle gives Timothy the reassurance he needs. He cannot hope to guard the gospel treasure by himself; he can do it only "with the help of the Holy Spirit who lives in us."

There is great encouragement here. Ultimately, it is God himself who is the guarantor of the gospel. It is his responsibility to preserve it. We may see the evangelical faith, the faith of the gospel, everywhere spoken against and the apostolic message of the New Testament ridiculed. Do not be afraid! God will never allow the light of the gospel to be finally extinguished. In entrusting the deposit to our frail, fallible hands, he has not taken his own hands off it. He is himself its final guardian, and he will preserve the truth he has committed to the church. We know this because we know him in whom we have trusted and continue to trust.

2 Timothy 1

....

DISCUSSION GUIDE

OPEN

How has your response to the gospel matured since you first heard it?

STUDY

1. What do we learn about Paul and Timothy from the first part of this letter (vv. 1-8)?

2. What is attractive about the relationship between Paul and Timothy?

3. How could practicing what Paul says in verses 6-7 strengthen Timothy for his ministry?

4. How might Timothy's characteristics have been assets for—or handicaps to—effective ministry?

5. Why do you think Paul gave Timothy the command in verse 8?

6. In what ways are we tempted to be ashamed of Christ's name, other believers, or the gospel?

7. In verses 9-10, Paul sketches out some of the main features of the gospel of which Timothy was not to be ashamed and for which he must take his share of suffering. What key words and phrases describe this gospel?

8. How are the roles Paul mentions in verse 11 the cause of his suffering (v. 12)?

9. Consider what motivated Paul to endure such suffering as imprisonment (v. 12). When it's difficult for you to be a Christian, how can Paul's motivation encourage you?

10. In addition to not being ashamed of the gospel, Paul outlines Timothy's responsibility in relation to it (vv. 13-14). What was that responsibility?

11. Why do you think there was such a difference in how Paul's Asian friends reacted to his imprisonment (vv. 15-18)?

12. What examples do you see today of people like Paul mentions (negatively and positively)?

APPLY

1. How can we "guard the good deposit" of the gospel today?

2. How can you follow the example of Onesiphorus this week?

2 Timothy 2
No Pain, No Gain

❦

Handing On the Truth

2 TIMOTHY 2:1-2

> [1]You then, my son, be strong in the grace that is in Christ Jesus. [2]And the things you have heard me say in the presence of many witnesses entrust to reliable people who will also be qualified to teach others.

Timothy had been called to responsible leadership in the church not only in spite of his natural diffidence but in the very area where the apostle's authority was being repudiated. It is as if Paul says to him: "Never mind what other people may be thinking or saying or doing. Never mind how weak and shy you yourself may feel. As for you, Timothy, be strong!" Paul's call to fortitude is not a summons to Timothy to be strong in himself—to set his jaw and grit his teeth—but to be strong "in the grace that is in Christ Jesus." Timothy is to find his resources for ministry not in his own nature but in Christ's grace.

If the disloyalty of the Asian church made it imperative that Timothy should guard the truth with loyalty, the approaching death of the apostle made it equally imperative that Timothy should make arrangements for the handing down of the truth intact to the next generation. In this transmission of truth from hand to hand, Paul envisions four stages.

First, the faith has been entrusted to Paul by Christ. It is his by deposit, not by invention or tradition. It came by a revelation of Christ.

Second, what has been entrusted to Paul by Christ, Paul in his turn has entrusted to Timothy. This deposit consists of words that Timothy has heard directly from Paul. The reference to "many witnesses" shows that the apostolic faith was not a secret tradition handed on privately to Timothy, but a public instruction whose truth was guaranteed by the many witnesses who had heard it and who could therefore check Timothy's teaching against that of the apostle.

Third, what Timothy has heard from Paul he is now to "entrust to reliable people," of whom there are evidently some left among the many deserters of Asia. These must be primarily ministers of the Word whose chief function is to teach—Christian elders whose responsibility it would be to preserve the tradition.

Fourth, such teachers must be "qualified to teach others." The ability or competence that Timothy must look for in such teachers will consist partly in their integrity or faithfulness of character, and partly in their facility for teaching.

Here, then, are the four stages in the handing on of the truth that Paul envisions: from Christ to Paul, from Paul to

Timothy, from Timothy to reliable teachers, and from those reliable teachers to others. It is to be a succession of apostolic tradition, a transmission of the apostles' doctrine handed down unchanged from the apostles to subsequent generations and passed from hand to hand like the Olympic torch. This apostolic tradition, this good deposit, is now to be found in the New Testament.

Soldier, Athlete, Farmer

2 TIMOTHY 2:3-7

> [3]Join with me in suffering, like a good soldier of Christ Jesus. [4]No one serving as a soldier gets entangled in civilian affairs, but rather tries to please his commanding officer. [5]Similarly, anyone who competes as an athlete does not receive the victor's crown except by competing according to the rules. [6]The hardworking farmer should be the first to receive a share of the crops. [7]Reflect on what I am saying, for the Lord will give you insight into all this.

Paul's prison experiences have given him ample opportunity to watch Roman soldiers and to meditate on the parallels between the soldier and the Christian. Soldiers on active service do not expect a safe or easy time. They take on hardship, risk, and suffering as a matter of course. Similarly, if we are loyal to the gospel, we are sure to experience opposition and ridicule. The soldier must also be willing to concentrate. Soldiers on active service do not get "entangled in civilian affairs." What is forbidden the good soldier of Jesus Christ is not all "secular" activities, but rather the involvements which, though innocent in themselves, may hinder us from fighting Christ's battles.

Paul now turns to the image of the competitor in the Greek games. In no athletic contest of the ancient world (any more than of the modern) did a competitor give a random display of strength or skill. Every sport had its rules, always for the contest itself and sometimes for the preparatory training as well. No athlete, however brilliant, received "the victor's crown" unless that athlete had competed "according to the rules." The Christian is under obligation to live lawfully, to keep the rules, to obey God's moral laws. We are not under law as a way of salvation but as a guide to conduct. There is no crown otherwise, not because our law abiding could ever justify us, but rather because without it we give evidence that we have never been justified.

If the athlete must play fair, the farmer must keep on working hard, no matter how poor the soil or inclement the weather. Unlike the soldier and the athlete, the farmer's life lacks excitement and praise. Yet the first share of the crops goes to the hardworking farmer, who deserves it. To what kind of harvest is the apostle referring? First, holiness is a harvest. Many Christians are surprised that they are not noticeably growing in holiness. Is it that we are neglecting to cultivate the field of our character? Second, winning converts is also a harvest. Both the sowing of the good seed of God's Word and the reaping of the harvest are hard work, especially when the laborers are few. Souls are won for Christ by tears and sweat and pain, especially in prayer and in sacrificial personal friendship.

Paul has isolated three aspects of wholeheartedness that should be found in Timothy and in all those who seek to pass on the good deposit to others: the dedication of a good soldier, the law-abiding obedience of a good athlete, and the painstaking labor of a good farmer. Without these we cannot expect results.

Suffering: A Condition of Blessing

2 TIMOTHY 2:8-13

> [8]Remember Jesus Christ, raised from the dead, descended from David. This is my gospel, [9]for which I am suffering even to the point of being chained like a criminal. But God's word is not chained. [10]Therefore I endure everything for the sake of the elect, that they too may obtain the salvation that is in Christ Jesus, with eternal glory.
>
> [11]Here is a trustworthy saying:
>
>> If we died with him,
>>   we will also live with him;
>> [12]if we endure,
>>   we will also reign with him.
>> If we disown him,
>>   he will also disown us;
>> [13]if we are faithless,
>>   he remains faithful,
>>   for he cannot disown himself.

At first glance Paul's command to "remember Jesus Christ" seems extraordinary. Yet human memory is notoriously fickle. We are to remember Christ because he is the gospel, the heart of the good deposit. In particular, Christ is to be remembered as the one who is both "raised from the dead" and "descended from David."

The words "descended from David" imply his humanity, for they speak of his earthly descent from David. The words "raised from the dead" imply his divinity, for he was powerfully designated God's Son by his resurrection. "Raised from the dead" also indicates that he died for our sins and was raised to prove the efficacy of his sin-bearing sacrifice. "Descended from David" indicates that he has established his kingdom as great David's greater Son. These facts illustrate, from Jesus Christ's own experience, the principle that death is the gateway to life and suffering the path to glory.

"Therefore," Paul writes, "I endure everything for the sake of the elect, that they too may obtain . . . salvation." Paul's statement that the salvation of others is secured by his sufferings may astonish us. Yet it is so. Not that his sufferings have any redemptive efficacy like Christ's, but that the elect are saved through the gospel and that Paul could not preach the gospel without suffering for it.

Paul now quotes a current saying or fragment of an early Christian hymn. It consists of two pairs of epigrams which apply equally to all believers. The first pair relates to those who remain true and endure, the second pair to those who become false and faithless.

The death "with" Christ mentioned here refers to our death to self and to safety as we take up the cross and follow Christ. Only if we share Christ's death on earth will we share his life in heaven. Only if we share his sufferings and endure will we share his reign in the hereafter.

The second pair of epigrams envisions the dreadful possibility of our denying Christ and proving faithless. The words "he remains faithful" have been taken as a comforting assurance that, even if we turn away from Christ, he will not turn away from us. Yet "if we disown him" and "if we are faithless" are parallels, which requires that "he will also disown us" and "he remains faithful" must be parallels also. In this case his faithfulness when we are faithless will be faithfulness to his warnings. If he did not deny us (in faithfulness to his plain warnings), he would then deny himself.

The apostle Paul has been hammering home a single lesson. From secular analogy (soldiers, athletes, farmers) and from spiritual experience (Christ's, his own, every Christian's) he insists that blessing comes through pain, fruit through toil, life through death, and glory through suffering. It is an invariable law of Christian life and service.

The Unashamed Worker

2 TIMOTHY 2:14-19

[14]Keep reminding God's people of these things. Warn them before God against quarreling about words; it is of no value, and only ruins those who listen. [15]Do your best to present yourself to God as one approved, a worker who does not need to be ashamed and who correctly handles the word of truth. [16]Avoid godless chatter, because those who indulge in it will become more and more ungodly. [17]Their teaching will spread like gangrene.

Among them are Hymenaeus and Philetus, [18]who have departed from the truth. They say that the resurrection has already taken place, and they destroy the faith of some. [19]Nevertheless, God's solid foundation stands firm, sealed with this inscription: "The Lord knows those who are his," and, "Everyone who confesses the name of the Lord must turn away from wickedness."

Several facts are evident from Paul's exhortation to Timothy to aim to be an unashamed worker. First, the kind of work the Christian worker does is teaching. The worker is called to handle "the word of truth." Second, there are two kinds of workers. There are those who are "approved," who have been tested like coins or metals and passed the test; and there are those who are not approved because they fail the test. The former group do not "need to be ashamed," while the latter ought to be deeply ashamed of themselves. Third, the difference between these two categories concerns their handling or treatment of "the word of truth," the good deposit.

The verb *handles* in verse 15 literally means to "cut straight." How does Paul picture "the word of truth" that Timothy is commanded to cut straight? I think it is as a road needs to be cut straight through the countryside. Or possibly the metaphor is taken from plowing rather than from roadbuilding, so the image is that of plowing a straight furrow.

"The word of truth" is the apostolic faith. For us it is, quite simply, Scripture. To "cut it straight" or "make it a straight path" is to be accurate on the one hand and plain on the other in our exposition. The approved worker handles the Word with scrupulous care, staying on the path, avoiding the byways, and making it easy for others to follow.

The metaphor Paul employs to describe the bad worker is taken neither from civil engineering nor from agriculture but from archery. The word of truth is a target. The archer who shoots at this target will either hit it or miss it. If the archer misses the mark, the attention of the spectators will be distracted from the target, and their eyes will follow the arrow however widely astray it goes.

Paul's instruction to Timothy about such bad workers or false teachers is to "avoid" them. Such false teaching leads people away from God, and it spreads its infection in the community. We would be wise to ask ourselves regarding every kind of teaching both what its attitude is toward God and what effect it has on people. There is invariably something about error that is dishonoring to God and damaging to people. The truth, on the other hand, always honors God and always edifies its hearers.

Clean Instruments

2 TIMOTHY 2:20-22

[20]In a large house there are articles not only of gold and silver, but also of wood and clay; some are for special purposes and some for common use. [21]Those who cleanse themselves from the latter will be instruments for special purposes, made holy, useful to the Master and prepared to do any good work.

²²Flee the evil desires of youth and pursue righteousness, faith, love and peace, along with those who call on the Lord out of a pure heart.

There can be little doubt that the "large house" is God's house, the visible or professing church. But what are the "articles" or "instruments"? The use of the term elsewhere in the New Testament suggests that they are not simply members of the church but the church's teachers. I think the two sets of instruments in the great house represent true and false teachers in the church. Paul is still referring to the two sets of teachers he has contrasted in the previous paragraph. The only difference is that he changes the metaphor from good and bad workers to special and common vessels.

It would be difficult to exaggerate the privilege the apostle sets before Timothy. Indeed he extends it to all Christian ministers or workers who fulfill the condition of cleansing themselves. They will then be "made holy, useful to the Master," and "prepared to do any good work." No higher honor could be imagined than to be an instrument in the hand of Jesus Christ.

The master of the house lays down only one condition. The instruments he uses must be clean. The words "from the latter" must refer back to the instruments "for common use." We are to hold ourselves aloof from the kind of false teachers who deny the fundamentals of the gospel and have violated their conscience and lapsed into some form of unrighteousness. But Paul's condition is even more radical. What Timothy is to avoid, and what we are to avoid, is not so much contact with such people as their error and their evil. To purify ourselves "from the latter" is to purge their falsehood from our minds and their wickedness from our hearts and lives. Purity—of doctrine and of life—is the essential condition of being serviceable to Christ.

The apostle elaborates what he means in an outspoken appeal that is both negative and positive. Negatively, Timothy is to "flee the evil desires of youth." Positively, he is to "pursue" the four essential marks of a Christian: *righteousness, faith, love,* and *peace.* We must not miss the sharp contrast between the two verbs *flee* and *pursue.* We are to recognize sin as something dangerous to the soul. We are not to negotiate with it or linger in its presence; we are to get as far away from it as possible as quickly as possible. By contrast, we are urged to go in hot pursuit of moral righteousness and its attendant virtues.

We are both to run away from spiritual danger and to run after spiritual good. It is the ruthless rejection of the one in combination with the relentless pursuit of the other that Scripture enjoins upon us as the secret of holiness. Only in this way can we hope to be fit for the Master's use.

The Lord's Servant

2 TIMOTHY 2:23-26

> [23]Don't have anything to do with foolish and stupid arguments, because you know they produce quarrels. [24]And the Lord's servant must not be quarrelsome but must be kind to everyone, able to teach, not resentful. [25]Opponents must be gently instructed, in the hope that God will grant them repentance leading to a knowledge of the truth, [26]and that they will come to their senses and escape from the trap of the devil, who has taken them captive to do his will.

Again Paul changes the metaphor. The utensil in the house becomes a slave in the household. But before outlining the kind of behavior fitting to the Lord's servant, Paul sets the context in which the servant has to live and work.

The word translated "arguments" is normally used in one of two senses. It means either an "investigation" such as a legal inquiry or a "discussion" like a debate. If it is used here in this sense, it refers to some kind of philosophical investigation and could be translated "speculation." But if it is used in the latter sense, the allusion is to a "controversy." Perhaps there is no need to choose between the two meanings.

What is being prohibited to Timothy, and through him to all the Lord's servants and ministers today? We cannot conclude that this is a prohibition of all controversy. For when the truth of the gospel was at stake, Paul himself was an ardent controversialist. What is forbidden is controversies which in themselves are "foolish and stupid" and in their effect "produce quarrels."

These controversies are *foolish* because they are speculative. For the same reason they are *stupid*, literally "uninstructed" or "undisciplined," because they go beyond Scripture and do not submit to the intellectual discipline that Scripture should impose on us. They also inevitably "produce quarrels" because when people forsake revelation for speculation, they have no agreed authority and no impartial court of appeal. They lapse into pure subjectivism and so into profitless argument in which one person's opinion is as good (or bad) as another's.

By contrast, the fundamental characteristic of "the Lord's servant" is to be "kind to everyone" as well as "able to teach," endowed with a gift or aptitude for teaching, and "not resentful," that is, forbearing of people's unkindness. The servant's instruction will sometimes have to be negative as well as positive. The servant is called to correct error as well as to teach the truth; yet in doing so, the servant should not be "quarrelsome."

If the Lord's servants adorn their Christian teaching with Christian character, and if they are meek in their dealings with the wayward, then lasting good may follow. God himself, through such a gentle ministry, may perform a conspicuous work of salvation. Important as is the part played by the gentle servant of the Lord in correcting sinners, it is God who gives or grants them repentance, God who illumines their mind to acknowledge the truth, and God who liberates them from Satan's power.

2 Timothy 2

....

DISCUSSION GUIDE

OPEN

When is it hardest for you to be strong for the Lord, and why?

STUDY

1. Why do you think Paul told Timothy to be strong in "grace" rather than in something else, such as knowledge (v. 1)?

2. Being strong in grace will help Timothy pass on the gospel to others. What is the process of passing on the gospel Paul describes here (v. 2)?

3. What connections do you see between the three metaphors of a soldier, an athlete, and a farmer (vv. 3-7)?

4. What kind of soldier, athlete, or farmer are you?

5. What are the sources of Paul's confidence (vv. 8-13)?

6. How can these verses also give you confidence?

7. What various instructions regarding speech does Paul give in verses 14-19?

8. Why is negative talk such a problem for Christians?

9. How can we present ourselves to God as approved workers?

10. What are some examples of handling God's Word correctly?

11. How can we become vessels for God's special use (vv. 20-21)?

12. What did Paul tell Timothy to flee and pursue, and why (vv. 22-23)?

13. What qualities should characterize God's servant? Give a practical example of each quality in action.

APPLY

1. What do you need to pursue in order to be a more godly worker? Choose something to concentrate on this week.

9

2 Timothy 3

Living in the Last Days

❦

Terrible Times

2 TIMOTHY 3:1

¹But mark this: There will be terrible times in the last days.

Why does Paul introduce this chapter with such an emphatic command to Timothy to "mark this"? After all, active opposition to the gospel was already evident. Surely it is because Paul wants to emphasize that opposition to the truth is not a passing situation but a permanent characteristic of the age. We too should "mark this" or "understand this" and be quite clear about the perils and troubles that will beset us if we stand firm in the truth of the gospel.

Paul refers to "the last days." It may seem natural to apply this term to a future epoch, to the days immediately preceding the end when Christ returns. But biblical usage does not allow us to do this. It was the conviction of the New Testament authors that the new age (promised in the Old Testament) arrived with Jesus

Christ, and that with his coming the old age had begun to pass away and the last days had dawned. We are now living in "the last days." They were ushered in by Jesus Christ.

What follows in 2 Timothy 3, therefore, is a description of the present, not the future. Paul depicts the entire period between the first and second comings of Christ. This follows not only from the way the expression "the last days" is used in the New Testament; it is also plain from the fact that Paul does not give Timothy predictions about some future epoch that he will not live to see but instructions relating to his present ministry. Timothy is already living in "the last days" Paul refers to. And so are we.

In these last days, Paul adds, "there will be terrible times." The word was used in classical Greek both of dangerous wild animals and of the raging sea. This gives us an idea of the kind of seasons the church must expect in these last days. They will be both painful and perilous, hard to endure and hard to cope with.

Before we go on, we need to absorb Paul's words of introduction. We are living in the last days; Christ brought them with him when he came. These days will include seasons of peril and stress. We are to understand this, to be quite clear about it, and so to be prepared.

Disordered Love

2 TIMOTHY 3:2-5

²People will be lovers of themselves, lovers of money, boastful, proud, abusive, disobedient to their parents, ungrateful, unholy, ³without love, unforgiving, slanderous,

without self-control, brutal, not lovers of the good, [4]treach-
erous, rash, conceited, lovers of pleasure rather than lovers
of God—[5]having a form of godliness but denying its
power. Have nothing to do with such people.

The apostle employs nineteen expressions to describe the wicked
people who are responsible for the "terrible times" the church
must endure. Notice at once the first and the last phrases used.
The first says that they are "lovers of themselves" and the last that
they are not "lovers of God." In fact four of the nineteen expressions are compounded with "love," suggesting that what is
wrong with these people is that their love is misdirected.

There are fifteen other expressions, almost entirely descriptive
of the breakdown of people's relations with each other. The first
three enlarge on the meaning of self-love. The next five expressions may conveniently be grouped together, for they seem to
refer to family life and especially to the attitude some young
people adopt toward their parents. In an ideal society the relationship of children to their parents should be marked by obedience, gratitude, respect, affection, and reasonableness. In "terrible times" all five are lacking. The remaining seven words of the
catalog are obviously wider than the family.

All this unsocial, antisocial behavior—this disobedient, un-
grateful, disrespectful, inhuman attitude to parents, together
with this absence of restraint, loyalty, prudence, and humility—
is the inevitable consequence of a godless self-centeredness.
God's order, as plainly declared in his moral law, is that we love
him first, our neighbor next, and our self last. If we reverse the
order of the first and third, putting self first and God last, our

neighbor in the middle is bound to suffer. Only the gospel offers a radical solution to this problem. For only the gospel promises a new birth or new creation, which involves being turned inside out from self to unself, a reorientation of mind and conduct that makes us fundamentally God-centered instead of self-centered.

It may be a shock to discover that people who lack the common decencies of civilized society, let alone of God's law, can also be religious. But the Old Testament prophets and the Lord Jesus denounced those who simultaneously engaged in religion and injustice. The same thing is going on among the people Paul describes. They preserve the outward "form" of religion but deny its "power."

True religion combines form and power. It is not external form without power, nor does it emphasize moral power in such a way as to despise or dispense with proper external forms. It fosters worship, which is essentially spiritual, from the heart, but expresses itself through public, corporate services, and also issues in moral behavior.

Devious Teachers

2 TIMOTHY 3:6-9

> [6]They are the kind who worm their way into homes and gain control over gullible women, who are loaded down with sins and are swayed by all kinds of evil desires, [7]always learning but never able to come to a knowledge of the truth. [8]Just as Jannes and Jambres opposed Moses, so also these teachers oppose the truth. They are men of depraved

minds, who, as far as the faith is concerned, are rejected. [9]But they will not get very far because, as in the case of those men, their folly will be clear to everyone.

It is astonishing that the kind of people Paul has been describing, filled with godless self-love and malice, should not only profess religion but actively propagate it. Yet this was happening in Paul's time and still happens today. Their method was not direct and open; it was furtive, secretive, cunning. They were sneaks. Using the back door rather than the front, these tradesmen of heresy insinuated themselves into private homes. The women chosen as victims were morally weak, "loaded down with sins" and "swayed by all kinds of evil desires." The false teachers played on their feelings of guilt and of infirmity. These targeted women were also intellectually weak, "always learning but never able to come to a knowledge of the truth." In such a state of mental confusion, people will listen to any teacher, however specious.

As an example of spurious teachers, Paul now mentions Jannes and Jambres, the names (according to Jewish tradition) of the two chief magicians in Pharaoh's court when Moses and Aaron were trying to persuade Pharaoh to release the Hebrew slaves. "Just as Jannes and Jambres opposed Moses," so the Asian false teachers "oppose the truth." What truth? The truth taught by Paul and entrusted by Paul to Timothy. Thus the apostle Paul, naturally and without any apparent hesitation, puts himself on a level with Moses as one who also taught God's truth. Moses taught the law; Paul preached the gospel. Whether it was law or gospel, the teaching of Moses the prophet or Paul the apostle, these people were opposing and rejecting God's truth.

So Paul rejects the devious false teachers as people with "depraved minds," despite their claim to knowledge. He is confident that such people "will not get very far." Their false teaching may temporarily spread, but its success will be limited and transient. How can Paul be so sure? Because "their folly will be clear to everyone," as happened in the case of Pharaoh's magicians.

Today we are sometimes distressed by the false teachers who oppose the truth and trouble the church, especially by the sly and slippery methods of backdoor religious traders. But we do not need to fear. Error may spread and be popular for a time, but in the end it is bound to be exposed, and the truth is sure to be vindicated. This is a clear lesson of church history. Numerous heresies have arisen, and some have seemed likely to triumph. But today they are largely of antiquarian interest. God has preserved his truth in the church.

Paul's Example

2 TIMOTHY 3:10-13

> [10]You, however, know all about my teaching, my way of life, my purpose, faith, patience, love, endurance, [11]persecutions, sufferings—what kinds of things happened to me in Antioch, Iconium and Lystra, the persecutions I endured. Yet the Lord rescued me from all of them. [12]In fact, everyone who wants to live a godly life in Christ Jesus will be persecuted, [13]while evildoers and impostors will go from bad to worse, deceiving and being deceived.

Paul reminds Timothy not simply that he knows all about Paul's doctrine and conduct, as if Timothy were merely an impartial student or a detached observer, but that he has become a dedicated disciple of the apostle's. No doubt he had begun by taking pains to grasp the meaning of Paul's instruction. But then he went further. He made it his own, believed it, absorbed it, lived by it. Similarly, he doubtless began by watching the apostle's manner of life, but then he went on to imitate it. Because Paul knew himself (as an apostle) to be following Christ, he did not hesitate to invite others to follow himself. Thus in both belief and practice, in "teaching" and "way of life," Timothy became and remained Paul's faithful follower.

Paul goes on to list the characteristics of his life, in contrast to that of the self-lovers he characterized in verses 2-5. But why does he give us this catalog of his virtues and sufferings? Isn't it conceited for the apostle to put himself forward like this?

No, Paul is not boasting. He has reasons other than exhibitionism for drawing attention to himself. He mentions his teaching first and then goes on to supply two objective evidences of the genuineness of his teaching, namely, the life he lived and the sufferings he endured. These are good (though not infallible) tests of a person's sincerity and even of the truth or falsehood of the person's system.

The false teachers lived lives of self-indulgence, and it would be quite out of character to expect them to be willing to suffer for their views; they were too soft and easygoing for that. The apostle Paul, however, lived a consistent life of righteousness, self-control, faith, and love, and he remained steadfast to his principles through many grievous persecutions. In particular, he mentions the three Galatian cities Antioch, Iconium, and Lystra.

Timothy was a citizen of Lystra and possibly witnessed the occasion when the apostle was stoned by a hostile mob, dragged out of the city, and left in the gutter for dead, though from this and all other persecutions so far the Lord had rescued him. Perhaps Paul's courage under persecution had even played a part in Timothy's conversion.

Paul makes it clear that his experience was not unique. He sought to "live a godly life in Christ Jesus," loving and serving God rather than himself, and he suffered for it. Timothy had found the same thing. He had followed Paul's persecutions, first watching them, then discovering that he must share in them. Timothy could not be committed to Paul's teaching and conduct without becoming involved in his sufferings also.

Continue in What You Have Learned

2 TIMOTHY 3:14-15

> [14]But as for you, continue in what you have learned and have become convinced of, because you know those from whom you learned it, [15]and how from infancy you have known the Holy Scriptures, which are able to make you wise for salvation through faith in Christ Jesus.

Timothy has learned things and has firmly believed them. Now he must "continue" in these things with steadfastness and not allow anyone to shift him from his ground. Paul's clear command to "continue in what you have learned" rests on two simple and plain arguments. Timothy must continue in *what* he has learned, because he knows "from whom" he has learned it. His teachers include his grandmother, Lois, and his mother, Eunice, as well as the apostle Paul.

The first ground of Timothy's confidence, and the first reason why he should continue in what he has learned, is that he has learned it from Paul. Timothy has loyally followed the apostle's doctrine and example, and the teaching has been confirmed by Paul's consistent life and his fortitude in persecution. Timothy is confident of Paul and his teaching authority, and we can share his confidence. Paul's gospel is still authenticated to us by his apostolic authority.

Timothy has not only learned Paul's gospel and known Paul's authority. "From infancy" he has been instructed in the Old Testament Scriptures, presumably by his mother and grandmother, and he is therefore extremely familiar with them. He believes them to be divinely inspired, as Paul is about to say. So the second reason why Timothy must abide in what he has learned from Paul is its harmony with the Scriptures. This was Paul's consistent claim.

So then, the two reasons why Timothy should remain loyal to what he has come to believe are that he has learned it from Old Testament Scripture and from the apostle Paul. The same two grounds apply today. The gospel we believe is the biblical gospel, the gospel of the Old Testament and of the New Testament, vouched for by both the prophets of God and the apostles of Christ. We must heed the exhortation that Paul addressed to Timothy and abide in what we have learned because of this double authentication.

Paul notes that the sacred Scriptures are able to make Timothy "wise for salvation through faith in Christ Jesus." The

Bible is essentially a handbook of salvation. Its overarching purpose is not to teach facts of science, which people can discover by empirical investigation, but facts of salvation, which no exploration can discover but only God can reveal. Since the Bible is a book of salvation, and since salvation is through Christ, the Bible focuses its attention on Christ. Its comprehensive portraiture of Jesus Christ is intended to elicit our faith in him, in order that by faith we may be saved.

God-Breathed Scripture

2 TIMOTHY 3:16-17

> [16]All Scripture is God-breathed and is useful for teaching, rebuking, correcting and training in righteousness, [17]so that the servant of God may be thoroughly equipped for every good work.

Here Paul asserts two fundamental truths about Scripture. The first concerns its origin (where it comes from) and the second its purpose (what it is intended for).

First, his definition of "all Scripture" is that it is "God-breathed." The single Greek word indicates not that Scripture itself or its human authors were breathed into by God, but that Scripture was breathed or breathed out by God. *Inspiration* is a convenient term to use, but *spiration* or even *expiration* would convey the meaning of the word more accurately. Scripture is not to be thought of as already in existence when (subsequently) God breathed into it, but as brought into existence by the breath or Spirit of God. It is clear from many passages that inspiration, however the process operated, did not destroy the individuality or the active cooperation of the human writers. All that is stated here is the fact of inspiration, that "all Scripture is God-breathed." It originated in God's mind and was communicated from God's mouth by God's breath or Spirit. It is therefore rightly termed "the Word of God," for God spoke it.

Second, Paul explains the purpose of Scripture: it is "useful," precisely because it is inspired by God. Only its divine origin secures and explains its human usefulness. Paul goes on to show that the profit of Scripture relates to both core beliefs and conduct. As for core beliefs, Scripture is profitable for "teaching" and "rebuking." As for conduct, it is profitable for "correcting" and "training in righteousness." In our own lives and in our teaching ministry, do we hope to overcome error and grow in truth, to overcome evil and grow in holiness? Then it is to Scripture that we must primarily turn, for Scripture is "useful" for these things.

Scripture is the chief means God employs to bring "the servant of God" to maturity. The term may refer to those called to positions of responsibility in the church, and especially to ministers whose task it is, under the authority of Scripture, to teach and refute, to reform and discipline. In any case, it is only by diligent study of Scripture that the servant of God may become "thoroughly equipped for every good work."

2 Timothy 3

....

Discussion Guide

Open

Using five adjectives, describe contemporary people and the present world situation.

Study

1. Why is "having a form of godliness but denying its power" dangerous (v. 5)?

2. Identify some current examples of this religious description.

3. What did Paul mean by telling Timothy to "have nothing to do with" such people (v. 5)?

4. Describe some situations in which people are "always learning but never able to come to a knowledge of the truth" (v. 7).

5. Why do people like Jannes and Jambres ultimately fail (vv. 8-9)?

6. What key facts about himself does Paul want Timothy to recall (vv. 10-11)?

7. How would Paul's example encourage Timothy?

8. Why did Paul remind Timothy of what he already knew?

9. Why can people who live godly lives expect persecution (v. 12)?

10. From verses 15-17, how would you explain the authority of the Bible?

11. How is God's Word useful for both our core beliefs and our conduct (vv. 16-17)?

APPLY

1. Which of the negative attitudes and actions cited in 2 Timothy 3 do you need to guard against, and how can you do so this week?

2. How does this passage encourage you to press on in your beliefs and actions?

2 Timothy 4
No Regrets

❧

Preach the Word

2 TIMOTHY 4:1-2

> [1]In the presence of God and of Christ Jesus, who will judge
> the living and the dead, and in view of his appearing and
> his kingdom, I give you this charge: [2]Preach the word; be
> prepared in season and out of season; correct, rebuke and
> encourage—with great patience and careful instruction.

Paul's charge is addressed to Timothy, but it is applicable to
every person called to an evangelistic or pastoral ministry, even
to all Christian people. The essence of the charge is: "Preach the
word." Paul does not need to specify it further, for Timothy will
know at once that Paul means the body of doctrine he has heard
from Paul and that Paul has now committed to him to pass on
to others. The same charge is laid on the church of every age. We
have no liberty to invent our message, but only to communicate

"the word" that God has spoken and has now committed to the church as a sacred trust.

Paul lists four marks that are to characterize Timothy's proclamation of the word: *urgent*, *relevant*, *patient*, and *intelligent*.

All true preaching conveys a sense of the urgent importance of what is being preached. The Christian herald knows that these are matters of life and death. We are to proclaim the word whether the occasion is convenient or inconvenient.

The herald who announces the word is to "correct, rebuke and encourage." This suggests three different approaches: intellectual, moral, and emotional. God's Word speaks to different people in different situations, and we are to apply it relevantly.

Our responsibility is to be faithful in preaching the Word; the results of the proclamation are the responsibility of the Holy Spirit. We can afford to wait patiently for him to work. However solemn our commission and urgent our message, there can be no justification for a tactless or impatient manner.

Whether our proclamation is intended primarily to correct, rebuke, or encourage, it must be a doctrinal ministry. The Christian pastoral ministry is essentially a teaching ministry, which explains why candidates are required both to be orthodox in their own faith and to have an aptitude for teaching.

Paul does not issue his charge in his own name or on his own authority but "in the presence of God and of Christ Jesus," conscious of the divine direction and approval. His main emphasis, however, is not so much on the presence of God as on the coming of Christ. Paul is sure that Christ will make a visible "appearing" and that when he appears he will "judge the living and the dead" and consummate "his kingdom" or reign.

These three truths—the appearance, the judgment, and the kingdom—should be as clear and certain an expectation to us as they were to Paul and Timothy. They cannot fail to exert a powerful influence on our ministry. For both those who preach the word and those who listen to it must give an account to Christ when he appears.

Fulfill Your Duties

2 TIMOTHY 4:3-5

> [3]For the time will come when people will not put up with sound doctrine. Instead, to suit their own desires, they will gather around them a great number of teachers to say what their itching ears want to hear. [4]They will turn their ears away from the truth and turn aside to myths. [5]But you, keep your head in all situations, endure hardship, do the work of an evangelist, discharge all the duties of your ministry.

Although the apostle seems to anticipate that the situation will deteriorate, it is also plain from this paragraph and from what he has written earlier that such a time has already begun for Timothy.

What are these times like? One characteristic is singled out, that people cannot bear the truth. Paul expresses it negatively and positively, and he states it twice: They "will not put up with sound doctrine" but will accumulate teachers who "say what their itching ears want to hear." They cannot stand the truth and refuse to listen to it. Instead, they find teachers to suit the speculative fancies they are determined to wander into.

Notice that what they reject is "sound doctrine" or "the truth," and what they prefer is "their own desires" or "myths." They do not first listen and then decide whether what they have heard is true; they first decide what they want to hear and then select teachers who will oblige by toeing their line.

If people cannot bear the truth and will not listen to it, isn't it prudent for Timothy to hold his peace? Paul reaches the opposite conclusion. Timothy must not take his lead from the prevailing fashions of the day.

Now come four staccato commands that seem to be deliberately framed in relation to the situation Timothy finds himself in and to the kind of people he is called to minister to.

"Keep your head in all situations." Because the people are unstable in mind and conduct, Timothy is above everything else always to stay steady.

"Endure hardship." Whenever the biblical faith becomes unpopular, ministers are tempted to mute those elements that give most offense. Timothy must persist in teaching the truth and be prepared to suffer on account of his refusal to compromise.

"Do the work of an evangelist." Because the people are woefully ignorant of the true gospel, Timothy is to faithfully proclaim it. The good news is not only to be preserved against distortion; it is to be spread abroad.

"Discharge all the duties of your ministry." Even if the people forsake Timothy's ministry in favor of teachers who tickle their fancy, Timothy is to persevere until his task is accomplished.

Paul's four commands, although different in detail, convey the same general message. Those difficult days, in which it was hard to gain a hearing for the gospel, were neither to discourage Timothy nor to deter him from his ministry, nor to induce him to trim his message to suit his hearers, still less to silence him altogether, but rather to spur him on to preach. It should be the same with us. The harder the times and the more resistant the people, the clearer and more persuasive our proclamation must be.

Paul's Coming Departure

2 TIMOTHY 4:6-8

> [6]For I am already being poured out like a drink offering, and the time for my departure is near. [7]I have fought the good fight, I have finished the race, I have kept the faith. [8]Now there is in store for me the crown of righteousness, which the Lord, the righteous Judge, will award to me on that day—and not only to me, but also to all who have longed for his appearing.

Paul uses two vivid figures of speech to portray his coming death, one taken from the language of sacrifice and the other (probably) of boats. "I am already being poured out like a drink offering." So imminent does he believe his martyrdom to be that he speaks of the sacrifice as having already begun. "The time for my departure is near." *Departure* means "loosing" and could be used of untying a boat from its moorings. Before the great adventure of his new voyage begins, Paul looks back over his ministry of about thirty years. He describes it—factually not boastfully—in three terse expressions.

First, "I have fought the good fight." It seems probable that Paul again combines the soldier and athlete metaphors.

Second, "I have finished the race." Some years previously, speaking to the elders of the same Ephesian church Timothy now presides over, Paul expressed his ambition to do just this (Acts 20:24). Now he is able to say that he has done so.

Third, "I have kept the faith." In the context of this letter, which strongly emphasizes the importance of guarding the deposit of revealed truth, Paul is likely affirming his faithfulness. He means "I have safely preserved, as a guardian or steward, the gospel treasure committed to my trust."

So the work of the apostle, and to a lesser extent of every gospel preacher and teacher, is pictured as fighting a fight, running a race, and guarding a treasure. Each involves labor, sacrifice, and even danger. In all three Paul has been faithful to the end. Now nothing remains for him but the prize, which he terms "the crown" (or better "garland") "of righteousness," which is "in store" for him and will be given to him at the finish line "on that day."

The same vindication by Christ also awaits "all who have longed for his appearing." Longing for his appearing has no merit in itself, but it is a sure evidence of justification. The unjustified unbeliever dreads the coming of Christ (if the person believes in it or thinks about it at all). The justified believer, on the other hand, looks forward to Christ's appearing. Only those who have entered by faith into the benefit of Christ's first coming are eagerly awaiting his second coming.

Timothy's heart must have been profoundly moved by this exhortation from Paul, the old warrior who had led him to

Christ. The torch of the gospel is handed down by each generation to the next. As the leaders of the former generation die, it is all the more urgent for those of the next generation to step forward bravely to take their place.

Three Requests

2 TIMOTHY 4:9-13

> [9]Do your best to come to me quickly, [10]for Demas, because he loved this world, has deserted me and has gone to Thessalonica. Crescens has gone to Galatia, and Titus to Dalmatia. [11]Only Luke is with me. Get Mark and bring him with you, because he is helpful to me in my ministry. [12]I sent Tychicus to Ephesus. [13]When you come, bring the cloak that I left with Carpus at Troas, and my scrolls, especially the parchments.

Although Paul has finished his course and is awaiting his crown, he is still a frail human being with ordinary human needs. He feels terribly cut off and abandoned, exiled from the churches he founded and from the people in them he knows and loves. For a variety of reasons, a number of his close circle of traveling companions have left him or become separated from him. It is their fellowship that he misses more than anybody's.

The desertion of Demas is obviously painful to Paul. Instead of setting his love on Christ's future appearing, Demas "loved this world" (literally "age"). We do not know the details of his desertion. The other three people are not censured for their departure. Crescens "has gone to Galatia," and Titus has traveled to Dalmatia. No reason is given for these movements. However, Paul reports "I sent Tychicus to Ephesus." Tychicus has been sent on several responsible missions before, apparently carrying Paul's letters to the Ephesians, to the Colossians, and to Titus.

Apart from the solitary exception of Luke, Paul is alone in prison. He longs and asks for three things: for people to keep him company, for a cloak to keep him warm, and for books and parchments to keep him occupied.

First, companions. "Get Mark and bring him with you." Mark had been a deserter on the first missionary journey; later he was restored, and now he is "helpful" to Paul in his ministry. But above all Paul yearns for Timothy himself. The same apostle who has set his love and hope on the coming of Christ nevertheless also longs for the coming of Timothy. The two longings are not incompatible. Human friendship is the loving provision of God for humanity.

Warm clothing is also necessary to Paul. It is no doubt in anticipation of the coming winter that he feels the need of the extra warmth his "cloak" could give him. But who Carpus was and why Paul left his belongings with him in Troas, we can only guess.

The third necessity Paul mentions is "my scrolls, especially the parchments." The papyrus scrolls may have been writing materials or his correspondence or some official documents. The parchments may have been unused, but more probably they were "books" of some kind.

No doubt Paul enjoys the companionship and strength of the Lord Jesus in his dungeon. Yet the help he obtains from his Lord is indirect as well as direct. The same is true of us. When our spirit is lonely, we need friends. When our body is cold, we need clothing. When our mind is bored, we need books. To admit this is not unspiritual; it is human. We must not deny our humanity or frailty, or pretend that we are made of other stuff than dust.

The Lord Will Rescue

2 TIMOTHY 4:14-18

[14]Alexander the metalworker did me a great deal of harm. The Lord will repay him for what he has done. [15]You too should be on your guard against him, because he strongly opposed our message.

[16]At my first defense, no one came to my support, but everyone deserted me. May it not be held against them. [17]But the Lord stood at my side and gave me strength, so that through me the message might be fully proclaimed and all the Gentiles might hear it. And I was delivered from the lion's mouth. [18]The Lord will rescue me from every evil attack and will bring me safely to his heavenly kingdom. To him be glory for ever and ever. Amen.

Contributing to Paul's ordeal was the fierce opposition he had sustained to himself and his message from a metalworker named Alexander. We know nothing of the "great deal of harm" he did to Paul, except that "he strongly opposed our message." We may be sure that it was Paul's concern for the truth of the message, and not personal pique or vindictiveness, that led him to express his belief that "the Lord will repay him for what he has done."

Paul's "first defense" may have been the first hearing of his case. Roman law would have permitted him to employ an advocate and call witnesses. If ever an accused man needed help, it was then. Yet "no one came to my support, but everyone deserted me." We are not told what charges were laid against Paul. We do know from contemporary writers the kind of allegations that were being made against Christians at that time. They were supposed to be guilty of horrid crimes against the state and against civilized society. Whatever the case for the prosecution, Paul had no one to defend him but himself. Either because Christian friends could not or would not, he was unsupported and alone.

Yet like his Master, Paul knew that he was not alone. "The Lord stood at my side and gave me strength." Christ's presence at Paul's side and his gift to him of inward strength both fortified him to preach the gospel to all the Gentiles present and led to his rescue (at least temporarily) "from the lion's mouth." In one of the highest tribunals of the empire, before his judges and perhaps before the emperor himself, no doubt with a large crowd of the general public present, Paul preached the Word. In the future too, Paul goes on confidently, "the Lord will rescue me," not from death (for he expects to die) but "from every evil attack" outside God's permitted will. He will also "bring me safely to his heavenly kingdom," though Nero may soon dispatch him from his earthly kingdom.

What a superb illustration the apostle gives Timothy of his charge to "preach the word." Timothy has in past days followed Paul in his doctrine, conduct, and sufferings; he can safely follow Paul's example in this also. For in issuing the solemn charge to

Timothy to preach the Word and do it urgently, Paul has not
evaded the challenge himself. On the contrary, at a moment of
great personal loneliness and peril, he has set a shining example
of faithfulness to his calling.

Final Greetings

2 TIMOTHY 4:19-22

> [19]Greet Priscilla and Aquila and the household of One-
> siphorus. [20]Erastus stayed in Corinth, and I left Trophimus
> sick in Miletus. [21]Do your best to get here before winter.
> Eubulus greets you, and so do Pudens, Linus, Claudia and
> all the brothers and sisters.
>
> [22]The Lord be with your spirit. Grace be with you all.

Paul has not been left entirely friendless. He sends greetings to
his friends Priscilla, Aquila, and the household of Onesiphorus.
He sends Timothy items of news about two other mutual friends,
Erastus and Trophimus. He also mentions some Christians in
Rome who send their greetings; he names four, then adds "all
the brothers and sisters." Since Paul knows these names and can
send greetings from them to Timothy, it is likely that they are
believers who have visited him in prison.

Above all Paul yearns for Timothy himself. He has already
written "Do your best to come to me quickly" (v. 9); now he
writes "Do your best to get here before winter." If Paul is ever to
see Timothy again and enjoy his friendship, then Timothy must
come soon (while Paul is still alive) and in any case before winter
(when navigation would be impossible). Wonderful as are both

the daily presence of the Lord Jesus and the prospect of his coming on the last day, they are not intended to be a substitute for human friendships.

Knowing the sacred deposit entrusted to him, the imminence of his own martyrdom, the natural weaknesses of Timothy, the opposition of the world, and the extreme subtlety of Satan, Paul in this letter has issued to Timothy his fourfold charge regarding the gospel—to guard it (because it is a priceless treasure), to suffer for it (because it is a stumbling block to the proud), to continue in it (because it is the truth of God), and to proclaim it (because it is good news of salvation).

Timothy was called to be faithful in his generation; where are the men and women who will be faithful in ours? If we feel inadequate for the task, we need to consider the two brief expressions at the close of this letter: "The Lord be with your spirit. Grace be with you all." These are the last recorded words of the apostle. He prays, may the Lord be with you (singular), and may grace be with you all (plural). Paul's letter to Timothy was also directed to the whole church. It is directed to us today. Then, referring back to verse 18, we read "To him be glory for ever and ever. Amen."

It would be difficult to find a better summary of the apostle's life and ambition. He received grace from Christ and returned glory to Christ. In all our Christian life and service we should desire no other philosophy than this.

2 Timothy 4

....

DISCUSSION GUIDE

OPEN

If you died today, how do you think people would describe you?
How would you like people to describe you?

STUDY

1. Consider the key facts Paul cites about Christ in verse 1.
   How do they set the stage for his charge to Timothy in
   verse 2?

2. What do you think it would be like to receive a charge
   like this?

3. Verses 6-8 serve as an epitaph that Paul wrote for himself.
   As he faced his death, what aspects of his life did he choose
   to concentrate on in his epitaph?

4. How would Paul's attitude as he faced death encourage
   Timothy to endure?

5. Verses 9-16 are filled with Paul's sense of loneliness in
   prison. Yet why was he not bitter about being abandoned?

6. Demas had been one of Paul's close associates. What are some symptoms of loving this world as Demas did (v. 10)?

7. Paul mentions the circumstances of his first defense (vv. 16-18). How would his attitude toward those circumstances encourage Timothy?

8. Paul longed for and asked for three things: people, a cloak, and books and parchments (vv. 9-13). Why were these important to him?

9. To admit such needs is not unspiritual; it is human. If you were in Paul's situation, who and what would you long for?

10. How can Paul's example at the end of his life encourage you when your faith is tested or your friends abandon you?

11. Look again at verses 8 and 18. How would you like to claim the promises of these verses for your own life?

APPLY

1. What is the most important truth you have learned from the book of 2 Timothy?

2. How will you put this truth into practice this week?

Titus 1
Truth in Church

❦

Servant and Apostle

TITUS 1:1-3

> [1]Paul, a servant of God and an apostle of Jesus Christ to further the faith of God's elect and their knowledge of the truth that leads to godliness—[2]in the hope of eternal life, which God, who does not lie, promised before the beginning of time, [3]and which now at his appointed season he has brought to light through the preaching entrusted to me by the command of God our Savior.

Paul is both "a servant of God and an apostle of Jesus Christ." *Servant* is literally "slave," and "slave of God" is a title of great humility as one bought, owned, and directed by God. "Apostle of Jesus Christ," on the other hand, is a title of great authority, designating specially the Twelve and Paul, who had received a unique personal call, commission, authorization, and equipment from Jesus Christ himself to be his inspired messengers.

For what purpose had Paul become God's slave and Christ's apostle? To foster or nurture "the faith of God's elect and their knowledge of the truth that leads to godliness." Faith and knowledge are two fundamental characteristics of the people of God. Far from being incompatible, faith and knowledge, or faith and reason, belong together. Those who know God's name or revealed character put their trust in him, and they trust him because they know that he is trustworthy.

Consider "faith" first, as Paul does. God's people are believers, the family of faith. Yet there are degrees of faith, and we are to keep growing in faith. Our "knowledge" is also to grow, for it is part of Paul's apostleship to further or increase it. In particular, he has in mind our "knowledge of the truth," which "leads to godliness" or God-centeredness. Since truth comes from God, it leads to God. Any doctrine that does not promote godliness is fraudulent.

The third characteristic of the people of God is "the hope of eternal life." How is it that our Christian hope, in contrast to all secular hopes, is so reliable? It is because its object is eternal life and because our eternal life has been given a threefold guarantee by God himself: he "promised" it "before the beginning of time" because it is part of his eternal purpose for his people; he "does not lie," indeed he cannot; and "at his appointed season he has brought" it "to light" through Paul's message. Thus the promise, the character, and the gospel of God combine to guarantee the certainty of eternal life. We may marvel at Paul's grasp of time and eternity. God made his initial promise before time began; he has revealed it to the world at the right time through the gospel; and he will fulfill it when time comes to an end. In this way the worldwide preaching of the gospel throughout the historical process is the bridge that spans the two eternities of past promise and future fulfillment.

Appoint Elders

TITUS 1:4-5

⁴To Titus, my true son in our common faith:

Grace and peace from God the Father and Christ Jesus our Savior.

⁵The reason I left you in Crete was that you might put in order what was left unfinished and appoint elders in every town, as I directed you.

Paul gives two reasons why he "left" Titus "in Crete." The first was that Titus "might put in order what was left unfinished." Paul mixes his metaphors, since one puts in order what is disordered, while one needs to complete what is unfinished. In particular, because this was evidently the chief unfinished business, Paul left Titus in Crete to "appoint elders in every town," as Paul had directed him.

Before we consider the qualifications for elders, on which the apostle concentrates, this paragraph allows us to make four statements relating to the pastoral oversight of the church. Both the qualifications and the statements overlap with 1 Timothy 3:1-13.

First, the elder and the overseer are the same person. They are not two distinct church officers but the same people with distinct titles. *Elder* draws attention to their seniority, while *overseer* draws attention to their task of pastoral oversight.

Second, God intends each church to have a team of overseers. Titus was told to appoint "elders" in every town. This might mean a single elder in each house church, assuming there were several such churches in every town. But it could mean that there were several elders in each church. So the one-person pastorate (like the one-person band, in which one musician plays all the instruments) is not a New Testament model of the local church. It is in a team ministry in which room can be found for different people with different gifts and different specialties—ordained and lay, full-time and part-time, salaried and voluntary, elders and deacons, men and women.

Third, the main function of elders is to care for God's people by teaching them. Other references to elders refer to the ministry of the Word of God, which includes both teaching truth and refuting error.

Fourth, the selection of elders is a corporate responsibility. True, Paul told Titus to appoint the elders, and he laid down the conditions of their eligibility. But his emphasis on their need to have a blameless reputation indicates that the congregation would have a say in the selection process.

It was for this important task of appointing elders that Paul left Titus in Crete, for the main way to regulate and consolidate the life of the church is to secure for it a gifted and conscientious pastoral oversight.

Blameless in Two Ways

TITUS 1:6-7

> ⁶An elder must be blameless, faithful to his wife, a man whose children believe and are not open to the charge of being wild and disobedient. ⁷Since an overseer manages God's household, he must be blameless—not overbearing, not quick-tempered, not given to drunkenness, not violent, not pursuing dishonest gain.

We are immediately struck by the requirement of blamelessness. Of course this does not mean that candidates must be flawless, or we would all be disqualified. Rather the word means "without blame," "unaccused."

First, elders must be blameless in their marriage and family life. The phrase "faithful to his wife" is not intended to exclude either those who have never married or remarried widowers, but rather the polygamous and those who have remarried after divorce. More generally and positively, ministerial candidates must have an unsullied reputation in the whole area of sex and marriage.

The elder must also be "a man whose children believe." It is a solemn thought that parents are held responsible for the belief and the behavior of their children. Yet the logic is plain. Parents cannot be expected to manage God's family if they have failed to manage their own. An extension of the same principle may be that elders can hardly be expected to win strangers to Christ if they have failed to win those who are most exposed to their influence, their own children.

Next, elders must be blameless in their character and conduct. Paul first lists five negatives that relate to five areas of strong temptation: pride, temper, drink, power, and money. All five challenge us to self-mastery. The principle is that elders cannot control the church if they cannot control themselves.

"Not overbearing." Leadership roles bring prestige and power, and leaders are tempted to misuse these in order to get their own way and pander to their own vanity. Then they do not readily listen to either criticism or advice, but tend to lord it over other people.

"Not quick-tempered." Pastors are often obliged to minister to difficult and demanding people. Their temptation is to become irritable and impatient.

"Not given to drunkenness." Pastors may have to attend social functions at which wine is served. Not all are total abstainers, but all are called to temperance and moderation.

"Not violent." Pastors who have learned their leadership style from Jesus Christ will never ride roughshod over other people's sensitivities. They will lead by example not by force, and by humble service not by self-assertion.

"Not pursuing dishonest gain." What Paul prohibits here is not so much dishonesty of practice as greed of motive. It is right for Christian teachers to be supported by those they teach, but wrong for them to exploit this situation from love of money.

Candidates for the pastorate must give visible evidence in their behavior that they have been regenerated by the Holy Spirit, that their new birth has led to a new life, that their fallen passions are under control, and that the fruit of the Spirit has at least begun to appear and to ripen in their lives.

Positive Virtues

TITUS 1:8-9

> [8]Rather, he must be hospitable, one who loves what is good, who is self-controlled, upright, holy and disciplined. [9]He must hold firmly to the trustworthy message as it has been taught, so that he can encourage others by sound doctrine and refute those who oppose it.

After the possible vices of elder candidates, it is a relief to turn to the desirable virtues, which are largely self-explanatory. An elder must be "hospitable," welcoming into his home both church members and visitors; "one who loves what is good," a person of large charity and a supporter of all good causes; "self-controlled," having both a sober, sensible judgment and a disciplined lifestyle; "upright" in his dealings with people; "holy" or devout in his attitude to God; and "disciplined." This reference to self-control comes last in this list of Christian virtues, as it does in the fruit of the Spirit. Self-mastery is an appropriate pinnacle of the list, covering everything which has preceded it.

In regard to qualifications for the pastorate, the apostle moves on from their home and family, and their character and conduct, to their necessary grasp of the truth. Candidates for the pastorate are to "hold firmly to the trustworthy message as it has been taught," that is, the reliable apostolic teaching, and never let go. Why? Because they will need it in their teaching ministry. And what form will their teaching take? It will have two complementary aspects, namely, to "encourage others by sound doctrine and refute those who oppose it." To "refute" people is not just to contradict them but actually to overthrow them in argument. But neither of these ministries (instructing and refuting) will be possible unless the pastors concerned maintain their firm hold on the sure word of the apostles.

It is clear from this that elders are called essentially to a teaching ministry, which necessitates both a gift for teaching and loyalty to the teaching of the apostles. Only then will they be able both to instruct and exhort people in the truth and to expose, contradict, and confound error. The negative aspect of this teaching ministry is particularly unfashionable today. But if our Lord Jesus and his apostles did it, warning of false teachers and denouncing them, we must not draw back from it ourselves.

The pastorate is a public office, and therefore the candidate's public reputation is important. Hence the requirement in many churches today both of individual references and testimonials and of a public statement by the candidate, followed by a public opportunity for the congregation to challenge it.

Disruptive Teaching

TITUS 1:10-11

[10]For there are many rebellious people, full of meaningless talk and deception, especially those of the circumcision group. [11]They must be silenced, because they are disrupting whole households by teaching things they ought not to teach—and that for the sake of dishonest gain.

The reason Titus is to appoint elders in every town and to ensure that they meet the standards Paul lays down is that there are many false teachers who are leading people astray. When false teachers increase, the most appropriate long-term strategy is to multiply the number of true teachers, who are equipped to rebut and refute error.

Having given an ideal picture of true elders in their blamelessness, Paul now by contrast describes the false teachers. He begins to alert Titus to their identity, influence, character, and errors.

Paul first describes them as "many rebellious people." Unlike the faithful elders who "hold firmly to the trustworthy message," the false teachers refuse to submit to it. Next, they are "full of meaningless talk." Their teaching lacks health-giving substance. Worse than that, they are deceivers. Their talk not only fails to edify; it actively leads people astray. And "especially" Paul is referring to "those of the circumcision group." Later in this paragraph Paul will indicate that these were not the Judaizers who argued that circumcision was necessary to salvation, but a Jewish group obsessed with "Jewish myths."

These people "must be silenced," Paul writes. It is not only individuals who are being deceived; the false teachers "are disrupting whole households" (house churches?) "by teaching things they ought not to teach." In addition, they have an ulterior motive, namely, "dishonest gain." Paul has already told Titus that true teachers must be free of the motive of greed.

Because of their growing influence, there is a need to take action to stop them teaching. Whether Titus is to stop these people by argument or by discipline is not divulged, but it is clear that their destructive influence must be halted for the sake of the church in Crete.

False Claims

TITUS 1:12-16

> [12]One of Crete's own prophets has said it: "Cretans are always liars, evil brutes, lazy gluttons." [13]This saying is true. Therefore rebuke them sharply, so that they will be sound in the faith [14]and will pay no attention to Jewish myths or to the merely human commands of those who reject the truth. [15]To the pure, all things are pure, but to those who are corrupted and do not believe, nothing is pure. In fact, both their minds and consciences are corrupted. [16]They claim to know God, but by their actions they deny him. They are detestable, disobedient and unfit for doing anything good.

The Christian conscience is uncomfortable with stereotypes such as the one Paul quotes. We need to remind ourselves that Paul believed in the power of the gospel to change people, that some Cretans received the transforming Holy Spirit in Jerusalem on the day of Pentecost, and that the elders Titus is to appoint are themselves Cretans, who are certainly not liars but teachers of the truth. Titus's responsibility toward the false teachers is to "rebuke them sharply, so that they will be sound in the faith" and will not pay attention to merely human ideas. There is a positive purpose in all truly Christian rebuke. Paul's aim is not to humiliate the Cretans for being gullible but to rescue them from error in order to establish them in the truth.

Paul now exposes the fundamental errors of the false teachers and their disciples.

Their first and most basic error is that they pay attention to "merely human commands." They follow the ideas of human beings "who reject the truth" of God. They forsake divine revelation for human opinions.

Second, they have a false understanding of purity. Like the Pharisees, they prize external and ritual purity above the true purity, which is internal and moral. "To the pure, all things are pure," including of course the Creator's good gifts of marriage and food. But for those who "do not believe, nothing is pure. In fact, both their minds" (what they believe) "and consciences" (what they feel able to do) "are corrupted."

Third, "they claim to know God," boasting of their knowledge, "but by their actions they deny him." There is a fundamental dichotomy between what they say and what they are, between their words and their deeds. Usually professions and denials are opposites that exclude one another. We cannot profess what we deny or deny what we profess. To do so is the essence of hypocrisy. This is ritual without reality, form without power, claims without character, faith without works.

These three phenomena regarding the false teachers and their disciples provide us with three valid tests to apply to any and every system. First, is its *origin* divine or human, revelation or tradition? Second, is its *essence* inward or outward, spiritual or ritual? Third, is its *result* a transformed life or a merely formal creed? True religion is divine in its origin, spiritual in its essence, and moral in its effect.

Titus 1

....

DISCUSSION GUIDE

OPEN

When you are confronted with false ideas about Christ, how do you respond?

STUDY

1. What does Paul's description of himself and Titus tell you about them (vv. 1-4)?

2. How does Paul's introduction to his letter encompass the past, present, and future (vv. 2-3)?

3. Describe the "truth that leads to godliness" (v. 1).

4. Paul emphasized that elders must be blameless in a number of areas (vv. 5-9). What are they?

5. Why is blamelessness so important for church leaders?

6. What positive qualities of elders are highlighted (vv. 8-9)?

7. Whether or not you are a leader in the church, how well do you measure up against the standards Paul listed for Titus?

8. Having given an ideal picture of true elders, Paul by contrast described the false teachers in Crete (vv. 10-16). How did he describe them?

9. Why is the influence of false teachers dangerous?

10. How did Paul tell Titus to deal with the false teachers (v. 11), and why?

11. According to verse 16, how can you determine whether someone truly knows God?

APPLY

1. Look again at your answers to questions 6-7. In what specific areas do you need to improve?

2. What steps will you take this week to become blameless— that is, unable to be accused—in one or more of those areas?

12

Titus 2
Truth at Home

❦

For the Older People

TITUS 2:1-3

> ¹You, however, must teach what is appropriate to sound doctrine. ²Teach the older men to be temperate, worthy of respect, self-controlled, and sound in faith, in love and in endurance.
>
> ³Likewise, teach the older women to be reverent in the way they live, not to be slanderers or addicted to much wine, but to teach what is good.

As rational human beings made in God's image, we need to know not only how we ought to behave as Christians but also why. We certainly need instructions about the kind of people we ought to be but we also need incentives. What is Christian behavior? And what are its grounds? These questions belong to one another, and Titus 2 is an outstanding example of this double theme.

In addition to "sound doctrine," Titus is to teach "what is appropriate" to it, that is, the practical duties that arise from it.

For there is an indissoluble connection between Christian doctrine and Christian duty, between theology and ethics.

Titus's first concern is to be for older members of the church. They need special advice and encouragement. The older men are to receive two main exhortations, which may be summed up in the words *dignity* and *maturity*. That is, they are to exhibit a certain seriousness that is both appropriate to their seniority and expressive of their inner self-control. They should also be "sound" or mature in every aspect of their character, especially in the Christian virtues of "faith" (trusting God), "love" (serving others), and "endurance" (waiting patiently for the fulfillment of their Christian hope).

"Likewise," Paul continues, hinting at the closeness of the parallel, Titus is to "teach the older women." Three areas of Christian conduct are singled out for them. They are to be "reverent," living in a way befitting a holy person. They are strenuously to avoid two moral failures: they are "not to be slanderers" (backbiters or scandal-mongers) or to be "addicted to much wine." Positively, instead of using their mouths for slander, they are to use them "to teach what is good."

It is clear that Titus is not to be content with abstractions or generalizations. Instead, he is to lay down some concrete and particular duties for specific groups of people in the church.

For the Younger People

TITUS 2:4-6

⁴Then they can urge the younger women to love their husbands and children, ⁵to be self-controlled and pure, to be

busy at home, to be kind, and to be subject to their husbands, so that no one will malign the word of God.

    [6]Similarly, encourage the young men to be self-controlled.

Who are the older women to teach? Their own family no doubt,
but especially "the younger women." Note that although Titus is
himself to teach the older men and older women, and later the
young men, it is the older women who are given the task of
teaching the younger women. This policy makes special sense
when the elder is a bachelor, but it may also be wise if he is married.

    The older women are to urge the younger women "to love
their husbands and children." Love is the first and foremost
basis of marriage, not so much the love of emotion and romance,
still less of eroticism, but rather of sacrifice and service. The
younger women should also "be self-controlled and pure" and
"busy at home." It is not legitimate to base on this phrase either
a stay-at-home stereotype for all women or a prohibition of
wives being also professional women. What is affirmed is that if
a woman accepts the vocation of marriage and has a husband
and children, she will love and not neglect them.

    Next, younger women are "to be kind," perhaps in the context
meaning hospitable, "and to be subject to their husbands." This
subjection contains no notion of inferiority and no demand for
obedience, but rather a recognition that, within the equal value
of the sexes, God has established a created order that includes a
masculine headship, not of authority, still less of autocracy, but
of responsibility and loving care. One reason the younger women
are encouraged to comply with this teaching is "so that no one
will malign the word of God." Christian marriages and Christian

homes that exhibit a combination of sexual equality and complementarity beautifully commend the gospel; those which fall short of this ideal bring the gospel into disrepute.

"Similarly," Paul continues, perceiving a parallel between the younger men and the younger women in the self-control expected of both, "encourage the young men to be self-controlled." The young men are to be urged to develop one quality only, that of self-mastery. Doubtless Paul is thinking of the control of temper and tongue, of ambition and avarice, and especially of bodily appetites, including sexual urges, so that Christian young men remain committed to the unalterable Christian standard of chastity before marriage and fidelity after it. Some valuable lessons can be learned from this verse. First, self-mastery is possible, even in young men, since there would be no point in exhorting them to an impossibility. Second, encouragement is an appropriate means to secure such self-control, especially if it is the sympathetic, supportive exhortation of one young man to another within the solidarity of the Christian brotherhood. Third, such an encouragement must be accompanied by a consistent example, which is exactly what Paul comes to next, namely the example which Titus must set.

For the Elder

TITUS 2:7-8

> [7]In everything set them an example by doing what is good. In your teaching show integrity, seriousness [8]and soundness of speech that cannot be condemned, so that those who

oppose you may be ashamed because they have nothing
bad to say about us.

By nature we human beings are imitative. We need models who
give us direction, challenge, and inspiration. God has provided
us with more than the deceased models of Old Testament pa-
triarchs and New Testament apostles. He wants us to have living
models as well. Chief among these should be the elders of the
local church.

Titus is to influence the young men of Crete not only by his
example but also by his teaching. Teaching and example, the
verbal and the visual, always form a powerful combination. His
teaching is to have three characteristics: "integrity," "seriousness,"
and "soundness of speech that cannot be condemned."

Integrity literally means "uncorruptness" and may well allude
to Titus's motives in ministry. *Seriousness*, on the other hand,
clearly refers to his manner in teaching, while *soundness of speech*
means that the matter of his instruction must be wholesome and
true. Perhaps the most important emphasis here is that people
will not take serious subjects seriously unless there is a due seriousness in the preacher's manner and delivery.

Titus, then, was to combine purity of motive, soundness of
matter, and seriousness of manner, "so that those who oppose
you may be ashamed because they have nothing bad to say about
us." Note the similarity between the reason for Paul's counsel to
Titus and the reason for his counsel to young wives: "so that no
one will malign the word of God." Ungodly behavior hurts the
reputation of the gospel, while godly living affirms it and makes
it appealing.

For Servants

TITUS 2:9-10

> [9]Teach slaves to be subject to their masters in everything,
> to try to please them, not to talk back to them, [10]and not
> to steal from them, but to show that they can be fully
> trusted, so that in every way they will make the teaching
> about God our Savior attractive.

The instructions Titus is to pass on to household slaves concern
their work and their character. As for their work, they must "try to
please" their masters by their conscientious service and "not to talk
back to them" but to be polite and respectful. As for their character,
slaves are to be honest "and not to steal from" their masters.

Instead, slaves are to be dependable, "to show that they can be
fully trusted." The reason slaves are to be honest and reliable in
both work and character is "so that in every way they will make the
teaching about God our Savior attractive." Although forced labor
is demeaning to human beings, voluntary service—even by slaves—
is noble. So Paul chooses slaves as his example of how good behavior can actually adorn the gospel. The gospel is a jewel, and a
consistent Christian life is like the setting in which the gospel
jewel is displayed. As with his instructions to young women and
young men, Paul desires that the godly lives of Christian slaves will
attract people—most likely their own masters—to the gospel.

Three times in the course of these verses about the Christian
behavior of different groups, Paul reveals his concern about the
effect of the Christian witness on the non-Christian world. In
two of them he refers to Christian doctrine. Young wives are to

be chaste and loving in order that the Word of God is not maligned or discredited. Household slaves are to be honest and reliable in order that the gospel may be adorned.

Christian doctrine is salvation doctrine, a jewel called "the teaching about God our Savior." Either we give no evidence of salvation, in which case the gospel jewel is tarnished, or we give good evidence of salvation by living a manifestly saved life, in which case the gospel jewel shines with extra luster.

The Epiphany of Grace

TITUS 2:11-12

> ¹¹For the grace of God has appeared that offers salvation to all people. ¹²It teaches us to say "No" to ungodliness and worldly passions, and to live self-controlled, upright and godly lives in this present age.

Paul now moves on from duty to doctrine, from mundane duties to sublime doctrines. His usual method is to begin with doctrine and then go on to its ethical implications. Here the order is reversed. Paul has begun with ethical duties, and now he lays down their doctrinal foundation. Both approaches are legitimate, so long as the indissoluble link between doctrine and ethics is forged and maintained.

Paul grounds his ethical appeal on the two comings of Christ, which he calls his two epiphanies or "appearings." Verse 11 says that "the grace of God has appeared," and verse 13 will say that we wait for "the appearing." Both Christ's appearings have a saving significance. What has already appeared is the grace of

God that brings salvation, while what we wait for is the glorious appearing of our great God and Savior.

Of course grace did not come into existence when Christ came. God has always been gracious. But grace appeared visibly in Jesus Christ. It was brightly displayed in his lowly birth, in his gracious words and compassionate deeds, and above all in his atoning death. His coming was moreover an epiphany of saving grace, of grace that publicly "offers salvation to all people."

Now Paul personifies this grace of God. Grace the savior becomes grace the teacher. "It teaches us" or perhaps disciplines us. What does grace teach? First, and negatively, "to say 'No' to ungodliness and worldly passions." Second, and positively, "to live self-controlled, upright and godly lives in this present age." Thus grace disciplines us to turn away from our old life and to live a new one, to turn from ungodliness to godliness, from self-centeredness to self-control, from the world's devious ways to fair dealing with each other.

It was for this purpose that the epiphany of God's grace in Jesus Christ took place. It is not only that grace makes good works possible (enabling us to do them), but that grace makes them necessary (challenging us to live accordingly). The emphasis is on the necessity, not the mere possibility, of good works.

The Epiphany of Glory

TITUS 2:13-15

[13]while we wait for the blessed hope—the appearing of the glory of our great God and Savior, Jesus Christ, [14]who gave

himself for us to redeem us from all wickedness and to purify for himself a people that are his very own, eager to do what is good.

¹⁵These, then, are the things you should teach. Encourage and rebuke with all authority. Do not let anyone despise you.

He who appeared briefly on the stage of history and disappeared will one day reappear. He appeared in grace; he will reappear in glory. This future epiphany of glory is the supreme object of our Christian hope, "the blessed hope," that is, the hope that brings blessing. Paul calls it "the appearing of the glory of our great God and Savior, Jesus Christ."

Already at his first coming his glory was revealed in his signs and supremely in his death. Nevertheless, his glory was veiled, and many did not perceive it or even suspect it. So one day the veil will be lifted, his glory will make an epiphany, and we will see him as he is.

Since this will be the epiphany of the glory of "our great God and Savior," who at his coming will perfect our salvation, Paul reverts naturally to his first epiphany when our salvation was begun. He "gave himself for us" on the cross. Why? Not just to secure our forgiveness but also "to redeem us from all wickedness," liberating us from its bondage, "and to purify for himself a people that are his very own." This special people of God Christ died to purchase for himself is described as "eager to do what is good," literally "enthusiastic for good works." This is not fanaticism, but it is enthusiasm, so that we may live for him who died for us.

In this short paragraph the apostle brings together the first coming of Christ, which inaugurated the Christian era, and the second coming of Christ, which will terminate it. He asks us to look back to the one and forward to the other. We live in between times, suspended rather uncomfortably between the *already* and the *not yet*. The best way to live now in this present age is to learn to do spiritually what is impossible physically, namely, to look in opposite directions at the same time. We need both to look back and remember the epiphany of grace (whose purpose was to redeem us from all evil and to purify for God a people of his own) and also to look forward and anticipate the epiphany of glory (whose purpose will be to perfect at his second coming the salvation he began at his first).

We need to say to ourselves regularly the great acclamation "Christ has died; Christ is risen; Christ will come again." Then our present duties in the home will be inspired by the past and future epiphanies of Christ.

Titus 2

....

Discussion Guide

Open

From your lifestyle, what could a stranger discern about your beliefs?

Study

1. What is the "sound doctrine" of verse 1?

2. Paul gave specific instructions for five groups of people. Identify each group and summarize what Paul instructed Titus to teach them.

3. What instructions are given specifically for Titus?

4. Why did Paul take care to give all these instructions?

5. How can the way we live make the gospel either appealing or unappealing to outsiders?

6. What are the similarities and differences between the two "appearings" of Christ?

7. How do the two appearings of Christ motivate us to godly living?

8. Why is teaching the truth so important?

9. What charge did Paul give Titus at the end of this chapter, and why?

APPLY

1. How can you help a younger or older Christian this week?

2. How can you be a more godly servant (in whatever capacity, paid or volunteer) this week?

13

Titus 3

Truth in the World

❦

Attitudes Toward Outsiders

TITUS 3:1-2

[1]Remind the people to be subject to rulers and authorities, to be obedient, to be ready to do whatever is good, [2]to slander no one, to be peaceable and considerate, and always to be gentle toward everyone.

"Remind the people," Paul begins, for the teaching he is about to give is not new. The churches have heard it before. But there are many warnings in Scripture of the dangers of forgetfulness, and there are many promises to those who remember. What Titus is to remind the people about concerns their social relationships in the world, first to the authorities in particular and then to everybody in general.

Paul has already written to Timothy about the need to pray for those in authority; now he writes to Titus about our Christian duty to obey them. Not that Christian citizens can ever give the state an unconditional allegiance. That would be to worship the state, as in the emperor worship of the first century, which Christians recognized as idolatry. Nevertheless, Christian duty in principle is to submit to the state because the state's authority has been delegated by God. This means that our first loyalty is to God, and if our duty to him comes into collision with our duty to the state, our duty to God takes precedence.

It is not enough, however, for Christians to be law abiding; we are to be public-spirited as well, "to be ready" (eager, not reluctant) "to do whatever is good," whenever we have the opportunity. The emphasis on "whatever is good" clarifies our responsibility and limits it. We cannot cooperate with the state if it reverses its God-given duty, promoting evil instead of punishing it, opposing good instead of rewarding and furthering it.

From our Christian responsibility toward the leaders of the community, Paul turns to our relationship with secular society at large. How are believers to relate to unbelievers? It is essential to see that this is Paul's concern, for he begins with a reference to "no one" and ends with a reference to "everyone." He selects four Christian social attitudes that are to be universal in their application, two negative and two positive.

Negatively we are "to slander no one" and "to be peaceable," which in Greek has the idea of avoiding quarrels. We must neither speak against nor fight against other people. Positively, we are to be "considerate" and always "gentle toward everyone." There is to be no limit either to our humble courtesy or to the people we show it to.

Here then is a brief delineation of Christian behavior in public life. In relation to the authorities we are to be conscientious citizens (submissive, obedient, and cooperative), and in relation to everybody, regardless of their race or religion, we are to be conciliatory, courteous, humble, and gentle.

Because of His Mercy

TITUS 3:3-5a

> [3]At one time we too were foolish, disobedient, deceived and enslaved by all kinds of passions and pleasures. We lived in malice and envy, being hated and hating one another. [4]But when the kindness and love of God our Savior appeared, [5a]he saved us, not because of righteous things we had done, but because of his mercy.

It is not enough to affirm that the grace of God that brings salvation has appeared to all people; we must be able to say that he saved "us," even that he saved "me." It is not just history that raises our expectations; it is experience. Without a personal experience of salvation we lack the right, the incentive, and the confidence to teach social ethics to others.

Paul now begins a condensed but comprehensive account of salvation. In the Greek, verses 4-7 are a single long sentence, which Paul may have taken from an early Christian creed. The whole sentence hinges on the main verb "he saved us." It is perhaps the fullest statement of salvation in the New Testament.

The apostle supplies an unsavory picture of the state and conduct of unregenerate people. In doing so, he discloses what we ourselves used to be like, and it is no exaggeration.

"At one time we too were foolish, disobedient." In other words, we were both mentally and morally depraved. We lacked sense and sensibility.

We were "deceived and enslaved by all kinds of passions and pleasures." Both verbs indicate that we were the victims of evil forces we could not control. Doubtless Paul alludes to the Evil One, that arch-deceiver who blinds people's minds and that arch-tyrant who takes people captive. We were his dupes and his slaves.

"We lived in malice and envy," which are very ugly twins. *Malice* is wishing people evil, while *envy* is resenting and coveting their good. Both disrupt human relationships.

We were "being hated and hating one another." The hostility we experienced in our relationships was reciprocal.

If we were truly deceived and enslaved, one thing is obvious: we could not save ourselves. Paul supplies God's solution: "he saved us." He rescued us from our former bondage and changed us into new people. Salvation originated in the heart of "God our Savior." It is because of his kindness, love, mercy, and grace that he intervened on our behalf. He took the initiative, he came after us, and he rescued us from our hopeless predicament.

God saves us not because of his mercy alone, however, but because of what his mercy led him to do in the sending of his Son. His attribute of mercy is indeed the source of our salvation; his deed of mercy in Christ is its ground. The basis of our salvation is not our works of righteousness but his work of mercy in the cross.

Heirs with Hope

TITUS 3:5b-7

> [5b]He saved us through the washing of rebirth and renewal by the Holy Spirit, [6]whom he poured out on us generously through Jesus Christ our Savior, [7]so that, having been justified by his grace, we might become heirs having the hope of eternal life.

Paul has already stated that God saved us "because of his mercy," that is, because of his merciful deed (the ground of our salvation); on the other hand, "he saved us through the washing of rebirth and renewal by the Holy Spirit" (the means of our salvation).

"Washing" is almost certainly a reference to water baptism. This does not mean that Paul taught baptismal regeneration. Most Protestant churches think of baptism as an outward sign of an inward cleansing from sins and of new birth by the Holy Spirit. But they do not confuse the sign (baptism) with the thing signified (salvation).

"Rebirth" translates a word that Jesus used of the final renewal of all things. Here, however, the new birth envisioned is individual rather than cosmic. It speaks of a radical new beginning. *Renewal* may be synonymous with "rebirth," the repetition being used for rhetorical effect, or it may refer to the process of moral renovation or transformation, which follows the new birth.

"The Holy Spirit" is of course the agent through whom we are reborn and renewed and whom God "poured out on us generously through Jesus Christ our Savior." The statement that the Spirit was "poured out on" us denotes our personal share in the Pentecostal gift.

Paul's complex statement could be paraphrased that "God saved us through a rebirth and renewal which were outwardly dramatized in our baptism but inwardly effected by the Holy Spirit." Or, reversing the order, "God generously poured the Holy Spirit on us; this outpoured Spirit has inwardly regenerated and renewed us (or has regenerated us and is renewing us), and all this was outwardly and visibly signified and sealed to us in our baptism."

Salvation means more than an inward rebirth and renewal, however. It also includes "having been justified by his grace." *Justification* means that God declares us righteous through the sin-bearing death of his Son; *regeneration* means that he makes us righteous through the indwelling power of his Spirit. God never justifies people without at the same time regenerating them, and he never regenerates them without justifying them. The work of Christ in justification and the work of the Spirit in regeneration are simultaneous.

The goal of our salvation is that "we might become heirs having the hope of eternal life." As his designated heirs, we cherish the sure expectation that one day we will receive our full inheritance in heaven, namely, "eternal life," an unclouded fellowship with God. Our hope for this fullness of life is secure because it rests on God's promise.

Excellent and Profitable

TITUS 3:8

> [8]This is a trustworthy saying. And I want you to stress these things, so that those who have trusted in God may

be careful to devote themselves to doing what is good.
These things are excellent and profitable for everyone.

Paul will not leave the subject of salvation without underlining the indispensable necessity of good works in those who profess to have been saved. He tells Titus, "I want you to stress these things" (that is, the essential ingredients of salvation), "so that those who have trusted in God" (and so have been saved by faith) "may be careful to devote themselves to doing what is good."

What kind of good deeds does the apostle have in mind? The reference seems to be generally to good works of righteousness and love. Good works are not the ground of salvation, but they are its necessary fruit and evidence. They are "excellent and profitable for everyone."

We are now in a position to summarize the six essential ingredients of salvation. Its need is our sin, guilt, and slavery; its source is God's gracious lovingkindness; its ground is not our merit but God's mercy in the cross; its means is the regenerating and renewing work of the Holy Spirit, signified in baptism; its goal is our final inheritance of eternal life; and its evidence is our diligent practice of good works.

Note what a balanced and comprehensive account of salvation Paul gives us. Here are the three persons of the Trinity together engaged in securing our salvation: the love of God the Father, who took the initiative; the death of God the Son, in whom God's grace and mercy appeared; and the inward work of God the Holy Spirit, by whom we are reborn and renewed.

Here too are the three tenses of salvation. The past is justification and regeneration. The present is a new life of good works in the power of the Spirit. The future is the inheritance of eternal life, which will one day be ours.

Avoid Foolish Controversies

TITUS 3:9-11

[9]But avoid foolish controversies and genealogies and arguments and quarrels about the law, because these are unprofitable and useless. [10]Warn a divisive person once, and then warn them a second time. After that, have nothing to do with them. [11]You may be sure that such people are warped and sinful; they are self-condemned.

So far in Titus 3, Paul has done two things. First, he has told Titus to remind the Christians in his care to be conscientious citizens (submissive, obedient, and public spirited) and to live consistent lives of peace, courtesy, and gentleness. Second, he has elaborated on the doctrine of salvation and so given Titus a ground for confidence that the people in his charge can be changed, so as to live the new life to which they are summoned.

Paul concludes his letter with a cluster of miscellaneous messages. What unites them is that they are all requests or instructions to Titus to do something.

Titus is to "avoid foolish controversies," but this cannot be taken as a prohibition of all theological controversy. Jesus himself was in constant debate with the religious leaders of his day. Paul was also drawn into controversy over the gospel and could not avoid it. So not all controversy is banned, but only "foolish" controversies. The word could mean "speculations." Its other occurrences suggest that Paul is contrasting the false teachers' speculative fancies with God's revealed truth.

The other three errors are "genealogies," "arguments," and "quarrels about the law." The references to genealogies and to the law show that a Jewish debate is in view. It is evident that Paul regarded the false teachers' treatment of the Old Testament as frivolous. Their speculations also led to "arguments" and "quarrels" or squabbles about the law.

Whereas Paul has pronounced good works as "excellent and profitable," foolish controversies are "unprofitable and useless." They are pointless and futile; they get you nowhere.

Stubbornly divisive people are to be disciplined in three stages, beginning with two clear warnings. "Warn a divisive person once, and then warn them a second time." Only then, if the offender remains unrepentant and refuses the opportunity of forgiveness and restoration, is the person to be rejected. "Have nothing to do with them." It is not plain whether this refers to a formal excommunication or to a social ostracism. Yet it is right to repudiate such a person. For after two warnings and two refusals, "you may be sure that such people are warped and sinful." An offender is to be given successive opportunities to repent; repudiation is to be the very last resort.

Grace Be with You

TITUS 3:12-15

[12]As soon as I send Artemas or Tychicus to you, do your best to come to me at Nicopolis, because I have decided

to winter there. [13]Do everything you can to help Zenas the lawyer and Apollos on their way and see that they have everything they need. [14]Our people must learn to devote themselves to doing what is good, in order to provide for urgent needs and not live unproductive lives.

[15]Everyone with me sends you greetings. Greet those who love us in the faith.

Grace be with you all.

Paul shares with Titus his intention to send someone to Crete who will be competent to take Titus's place and so free him to join Paul. Of Artemas we know nothing; nobody of that name appears elsewhere in the New Testament. Tychicus, on the other hand, is mentioned on five other occasions, and Paul evidently had great confidence in him. "As soon as" Artemas or Tychicus arrives in Crete and has been able to take over responsibility for the churches, Titus is to do his best to join Paul at Nicopolis, where Paul plans to spend the winter. Several towns with the name of Nicopolis have been identified, but this one is apparently on the west coast of Greece.

It seems likely that Paul has entrusted to Zenas and Apollos the task of carrying his letter to Titus. Once they have fulfilled their commission, they are to be sent on their way with all necessary supplies for their onward journey. "Our people" must demonstrate that they truly belong to Paul's following by giving themselves to good works and providing for the needs of others.

Titus must first receive the greetings sent to him by Paul and everyone with him. Then he is to convey Paul's greetings to others. These two-way greetings are an expression of how our common faith binds God's people together in love.

At the end of his letters, it was the apostle's custom to take the pen from his scribe and write a personal greeting. This commonly included the word *grace*, which succinctly expressed his message. He refers to the grace that issues from the Father and the Son, which made its historical epiphany in Christ, and by which we have been justified. So as he pronounces his benediction, Paul looks beyond Titus to all members of the Cretan churches, indeed to all who would later read his letter, including us: "Grace be with you all."

Titus 3

....

DISCUSSION GUIDE

OPEN

If someone followed you around for a week, how would that person describe your relationship with the world?

STUDY

1. How should we relate to rulers and others in authority over us (v. 1)? Give a practical example of obeying each instruction.

2. Paul moved from our Christian responsibility toward the leaders of the community to our relationship with everybody in the community (v. 2). How should we relate to unbelievers in general? Give a practical example of each action.

3. In verse 3, the person who does not know Christ is described in harsh terms. How accurately do Paul's words describe your pre-Christian life?

4. How do you react to seeing a person without Christ described in this way?

5. According to verses 4-7, how did God save us?

6. In what senses are the good works of Christians "excellent and profitable for everyone" (v. 8)?

7. What is the relationship between God's grace in salvation and our good works?

8. After telling Titus to stress the truth of salvation (v. 8), Paul told him some things to avoid (v. 9). What are the dangers of each one?

9. Paul gave specific instructions regarding a divisive person (vv. 10-11). Compare Paul's instructions with the way you usually respond to divisive people.

10. Consider the ways that Paul wanted Titus to help him (vv. 12-15). What do his instructions indicate about their relationship?

11. Why is it important for believers to help each other in practical ways?

12. When have you been especially grateful for the help of other Christians?

APPLY

1. Evaluate yourself in relation to good works. What is one specific way you can live for the benefit of others?

2. Paul wrote to Timothy and Titus to encourage them as well as to instruct them. Consider people you can communicate with this week to either encourage them or instruct them, or both. Make specific plans to do that.

Guidelines for Leaders

My grace is sufficient for you.

2 CORINTHIANS 12:9

❧

If leading a small group is something new for you, don't worry. These sessions are designed to flow naturally and be led easily. You may even find that the studies seem to lead themselves!

This study guide is flexible. You can use it with a variety of groups—students, professionals, coworkers, friends, neighborhood or church groups. Each study takes forty-five to sixty minutes in a group setting.

You don't need to be an expert on the Bible or a trained teacher to lead a small group. These guides are designed to facilitate a group's discussion, not a leader's presentation. Guiding group members to discover together what the Bible has to say and to listen together for God's guidance will help them remember much more than a lecture would.

There are some important facts to know about group dynamics and encouraging discussion. The suggestions that follow should equip you to effectively and enjoyably fulfill your role as leader.

PREPARING FOR THE STUDY

1. Ask God to help you understand and apply the passage in your own life. Unless this happens, you will not be prepared to lead others. Pray too for the various members of the group. Ask God to open your hearts to the message of his Word and motivate you to action.

2. Read the introduction to the entire guide to get an overview of the topics that will be explored. *The Message of 1 Timothy & Titus* and *The Message of 2 Timothy* will give you more detailed information on the text. These can help you deal with answers to tough questions about the text and its context that could come up in discussion.

3. As you begin each study, read and reread the assigned Bible passage to familiarize yourself with it.

4. Carefully work through each question in the study. Spend time in meditation and reflection as you consider how to respond.

5. Write your thoughts and responses. This will help you to express your understanding of the passage clearly.

6. It may help to have a Bible dictionary handy. Use it to look up any unfamiliar words, names, or places.

7. Reflect seriously on how you need to apply the Scripture to your life. Remember that the group members will follow

your lead in responding to the studies. They will not go any deeper than you do.

LEADING THE STUDY

1. At the beginning of your first time together, explain that these studies are meant to be discussions, not lectures. Encourage the members of the group to participate. However, do not put pressure on those who may be hesitant to speak—especially during the first few sessions.

2. Be sure that everyone in your group has a book. Encourage the group to prepare beforehand for each discussion by reading the introduction to the book and the readings for each section.

3. Begin each study on time. Open with prayer, asking God to help the group to understand and apply the passage.

4. Discuss the "Open" question before the Bible passage is read. The "Open" question introduces the theme of the study and helps group members begin to open up, and can reveal where our thoughts and feelings need to be transformed by Scripture. Reading the passage first could tend to color the honest reactions people might otherwise give—because they are, of course, supposed to think the way the Bible does. Encourage as many members as possible to respond to the "Open" question, and be ready to get the discussion going with your own response.

5. Have a group member read aloud the passage to be studied as indicated in the guide.

6. The study questions are designed to be read aloud just as they are written. You may, however, prefer to express them in your own words. There may be times when it is appropriate to deviate from the discussion guide. For example, a question may have already been answered. If so, move on to the next question. Or someone may raise an important question not covered in the guide. Take time to discuss it, but try to keep the group from going off on tangents.

7. Avoid answering your own questions. An eager group quickly becomes passive and silent if members think the leader will do most of the talking. If necessary, repeat or rephrase the question until it is clearly understood, or refer to the commentary woven into the guide to clarify the context or meaning.

8. Don't be afraid of silence in response to the discussion questions. People may need time to think about the question before formulating their answers.

9. Don't be content with just one answer. Ask, "What do the rest of you think?" or "Anything else?" until several people have given answers to the question.

10. Try to be affirming whenever possible. Affirm participation. Never reject an answer; if it is clearly off-base, ask, "Which verse led you to that conclusion?" or again, "What do the rest of you think?"

11. Don't expect every answer to be addressed to you, even though this will probably happen at first. As group members

become more at ease, they will begin to truly interact with each other. This is one sign of healthy discussion.

12. Don't be afraid of controversy. It can be very stimulating. If you don't resolve an issue completely, don't be frustrated. Explain that the group will move on and God may enlighten all of you in later sessions.

13. Periodically summarize what the group has said about the passage. This helps to draw together the various ideas mentioned and gives continuity to the study. But don't preach.

14. Conclude your time together with prayer, asking for God's help in following through on the applications you've identified.

15. End on time.

Many more suggestions and helps for studying a passage or guiding discussion can be found in *How to Lead a LifeGuide Bible Study* and *The Big Book on Small Groups* (both from InterVarsity Press).

Reading the Bible with John Stott

- *Reading the Sermon on the Mount with John Stott*

- *Reading Romans with John Stott, volume 1*

- *Reading Romans with John Stott, volume 2*

- *Reading Galatians with John Stott*

- *Reading Ephesians with John Stott*

- *Reading Timothy and Titus with John Stott*

Also Available

The Message of 1 Timothy & Titus

The Message of 2 Timothy